Lighthouses of England and Wales

Lighthouses of England and Wales

Including the Channel Islands
and the Isle of Man

Derrick Jackson

Illustrated by the author

DAVID & CHARLES

NEWTON ABBOT   LONDON

NORTH POMFRET (VT)   VANCOUVER

ISBN 0 7153 6902 4
Library of Congress Catalog Card Number 75-18685

Set in 11 on 13 point Baskerville
and printed in Great Britain
by Biddles Limited Guildford
for David & Charles (Holdings) Limited
South Devon House Newton Abbot Devon

Published in the United States of America
by David & Charles Inc
North Pomfret Vermont 05053 USA

Published in Canada
by Douglas David & Charles Limited
132 Philip Avenue North Vancouver BC

DEDICATION

This book is dedicated to my wife, Kathleen, who has patiently followed me around the coast from lighthouse to lighthouse and typed the script of the book; and to Wendy and Mark who were very good while I climbed and photographed numerous towers. I hope they enjoyed the fresh air and have gained some of my enthusiasm for lighthouses.

Contents

Seamarks and Services

Lighthouses

Ever since man has sailed the sea he has looked for ways of aiding navigation and especially of guiding ships safely back to harbour. By day he can look for well-known landmarks, maybe a tree, church steeple or headland, but by night the mariner is blind. What better aid could there be at such times than for friends to light a bonfire, or put a candle in a cottage window? These lights often appeared in different places on different nights, however, and could not be relied upon until a decision was taken to have a light in the same place and a keeper to maintain it.

The Romans opened up the world with their armies and trade, and built two lighthouses facing each other across the strait at Dover and Boulogne. The Dover pharos can still be seen. Few lights were exhibited in medieval England, those that were being supported by the church and sometimes maintained by hermits. Such small lights existed at St Catherine's in the Isle of Wight, Spurn Head and the church of St Nicholas at Ilfracombe, and some church towers along the east coast also served this humanitarian purpose, notably at Blakeney in Norfolk and Boston Stump in Lincolnshire. All these lights were extinguished at the dissolution of the monasteries and England's coast was literally left in the dark. The earliest lights established after this period seem to have been at North Shields c1540 and Tynemouth c1550 where a coal fire was kept at the castle to aid coastal navigation. Generally, however, the building of lighthouses round the English coast was a slow process. Before 1700 there were only eleven, all on the south and east coasts. Work began just before the end of the seventeenth century on the site of what was to become one of the world's most famous lighthouses, the Eddystone, which was the forerunner of many true rock stations. Rock stations are those which are built on small islands or rocks at sea, but some land installations are classified as rock stations by reason of their inaccessability. Keepers' families usually live at land stations but rock stations are manned by (in most cases) two teams of three keepers who alternate a month's duty with a month ashore, or they may be unwatched and automatic.

Trinity House gradually assumed control of lighthouse maintenance and construction during the last quarter of the eighteenth century and the first half of the nineteenth, and the great period of lighthouse construction, 1870-1900, followed. Much credit must go to the intrepid Victorian craftsmen for the construction or modernisation of at least fifty stations during this time, including the building of rock towers at the Eddystone, Wolf Rock, Longships, Bishop Rock and Beachy Head. Similar advances were being made in Scotland and Ireland, and lighthouses are situated now at intervals of about twenty miles round Britain's coastline so that from seaward at least two lights are always in range.

Modern technology has made possible the siting of unmanned towers where formerly only lightships could be stationed, and predictable power sources and light-sensitive switching apparatus make automatic lighting and fog signals reliable.

Many offshore lights are serviced and the keepers transported by helicopter, and new stations such as the Royal Sovereign tower incorporate a helicopter pad.

A typical land station is white-painted, with black roof and green doors and windowsills, but the colour scheme may be varied to make the station conspicuous from seaward; a white tower is acceptable against a dark headland but not against chalk cliffs, where it might be banded or painted completely in red or black.

The location of a lighthouse is governed by the sea area to be covered and the height of the tower by the range required. The lights shown are all warnings, but some can be defined as landfall lights — those which enable a ship's master to confirm his course to port or near land, and which could be described as marine signposts. This function is to some extent fulfilled by lights marking rocks, shoals, sandbanks and otherwise dangerous waters. Guiding or leading lights indicate the bearing a ship must take in order to avoid danger, and a pair of them must sometimes be kept in line when an approach is being made through a narrow deep water channel. Some rock and island lights show all round the horizon; landfall lights may have a narrow arc of visibility; there may be a secondary light marking a hazard; in a few cases, part of the beam may be deflected ten or fifteen degrees from the horizontal for the benefit of aircraft (aeromarine lights).

Lightships

The first petition to establish a lightship (or light-vessel, an alternative name), in 1679, was ridiculed. Trinity House wanted to know how a small vessel could be held on station by hemp ropes alone, where a crew was to be found who would be willing to man it, and how effective it would be anyway with a few candles for its illumination. Their opposition was apparently well-founded. Shipowners did not agree, however, and a private adventurer named Robert Hamblin and his colleague David Amery stationed the world's first lightship at the Nore, at the entrance to the Thames, in 1732 and levied tolls on passing ships for maintenance. It drifted off station many times but by now the value of the navigational aid had been established and other lightships were launched, the first four years later to mark the Dudgeon Shoal at the entrance to the Wash. The next fifty years were marred by inertia, but Trinity House responded to pressure for a lightship on Owers Shoal, off the Sussex coast, in the path of ships making for Portsmouth; then, following a storm disaster off the Norfolk coast in 1789 when twenty-three ships were lost, twenty more driven ashore and 600 seaman drowned, they placed a lightship on the Newarp Sand.

No area was as treacherous as the Goodwin Sands, the great 'shippe swallower' of medieval times, lying six miles off the Kent coast. At first dismissing petitions to light the Goodwins, Trinity House were obliged to reconsider their objections with the result that a lightship was commissioned a few years later and, over the next three-quarters of a century, several more were placed there. At low tide, lightships' crews can walk and play games on the sand, but the Goodwins are still a constant navigation hazard in bad weather; lightships were swept from their moorings in 1929 and 1954 and were lost with their crews.

Today, a fleet of about thirty with several reserve vessels, is maintained, concentrated for the main part at strategic navigational points along the east coast of England; some are well offshore.

A modern lightship is functionally designed; it has no engine and is towed into position and moored with chains. Its light is carried about forty feet above the waterline, and each vessel has its unique light characteristic which enables it to be identified. By day, it is distinguished by its red hull and lantern and name painted in large white letters on both sides of the hull. A crew of eleven mans each vessel, seven being on board at one time.

The current annual maintenance cost for each vessel tops £30,000 and this, together with the lightships' vulnerability to the weather and other shipping, has led Trinity House to explore means of replacing them by automatic buoys, notably LANBY (large automatic navigation buoy), which is capable of running without attention for six months and costs in maintenance approximately one-tenth of the amount needed for a lightship. LANBY is a steel construction of discus shape 40ft in diameter and 7½ft deep, and carries a central 40ft mast with light and fog signal.

The coastguard service

The original purpose of the coastguard service was to prevent smuggling, help ships in distress, and make signals to vessels seen to be steering a dangerous course when approaching land. The nineteenth-century establishment operated from small stations supplied with life-saving apparatus, and the government placed forty-five mortar stations under the care of the coastguard or 'Preventive Service' in 1814 — mortar stations contained rockets connected by hawser to lifebuoys.

The coastguard's life-saving function grew in importance and effectiveness with the introduction of telecommunication, and a 1903 Admiralty regulation charged officers to ensure constant attendance at the telephone; where this was impossible, 'a competent person (preferably the wife of one of the Coast Guard men) may be engaged for the duty, and paid . . . '

There are now about 400 coastguard stations manned by a total of about 600 officers. Each station is in contact with the lifeboat service and the Air Rescue Co-ordination Centres; a lifeboat or a helicopter can thus be called to the aid of a ship in distress, even though the ARCCs are concerned mainly with aircraft which have crashed into the sea around the United Kingdom. Contact is maintained through the coastal radio stations (CRS), which monitor distress signals and inform the rescue services and other ships in the area. The coastguard relays the message to the local secretary of the RNLI who decides whether a lifeboat is needed.

The pilot service

The job of the pilot is to guide ships in narrow or difficult waters where local knowledge is necessary; a pilot has to be licensed by Trinity House, and in a small port may be a fisherman or boatman. In large ports like London and Southampton a pilot must hold a master's (captain's) certificate allowing him to take charge of a foreign-going ship. The pilot does not usually steer the ship but gives orders to the helmsman, and is paid by the ship-owner for his services. Pilots are self-employed, and it is the custom at some ports for earnings to be pooled.

In busy seaways, pilots provide a permanent service based on a pilot cutter, a small vessel which is instantly ready to get under way when an incoming ship indicates by radio or signal flags that a pilot is required. A ship under a pilot's control shows a red and white flag.

Like lightships, cutters are expensive to build and maintain, and are being replaced where possible by fast shore-based launches; pilots are thus relieved of unproductive hours spent waiting at sea for ships needing their services.

Of the 800 or so Trinity House pilots, about 500 are based on the Thames.

The lifeboat service

The first known lifeboat, ordered from inventor Lionel Lukin and financed by the Crewe Trust set up sixty years earlier by Nathaniel, Lord Crewe, then Bishop of Durham, for the benefit of seafarers, was a converted fishing boat. It was fitted with air boxes for buoyancy and was reckoned to be unsinkable. The launching took place in 1786 at Bamburgh on the Northumberland coast.

The voluntary and humane service of lifesaving was becoming well established by this time, and in the north-east of England was inspired by the commitment of the dukes of Northumberland to the inauguration of an organised lifeboat system. Competitions for life-boat designs were sponsored, and two North Shields men built the *Original* in 1790; she saved hundreds of lives before being wrecked in 1840. The fourth duke's prize of 1851 stimulated a Great Yarmouth man, James Beeching, to design and build a self-righting boat of a type which continued in service into this century.

The first organised corps of lifesavers, the Volunteer Life Brigade, was founded at Tynemouth in 1846 to work under the direction of the coastguard; the seed had been sown forty years earlier by Sir William Hillary in his proposal for the National Shipwreck Society, later to become the National Lifeboat Institute (the RNLI today). In the course of its life, the organisation has saved over 87,000 lives and today rescues about 1,000 people a year.

It is maintained entirely by voluntary contributions; crews give their services free, and the only full-time paid members of the 150 or so stations are the mechanics.

Early lifeboats were propelled by oars; steam power was tried in the 1890s but the biggest step forward came in 1904 with 10hp petrol engines. Modern lifeboats are self-righting, and the recently introduced 70ft steel boats can remain at sea for several days and carry up to 150 survivors.

Another innovation, the inshore rescue boat, has proved its worth as a coastal patrol ready to attend to swimmers and small-boat sailors in trouble.

Trinity House

Three major authorities are responsible for maintaining aids to navigation in the United Kingdom and Eire: the Northern Lighthouse Board, Edinburgh; the Commissioners of Irish Lights, Dublin; and the Corporation of Trinity House, London. Trinity House has jurisdiction over erection or alteration of seamarks by the other two bodies.

The authorities are financed from dues paid by shipping, which make up the general lighthouse fund, administered by the Department of Trade.

Sixteenth-century mariners' guilds were centred on the ports of Hull, Newcastle, Dover, Scarborough, and Deptford Strond on the Thames, and were mainly responsible for pilotage in their areas and were the first to be approached with petitions for the building of seamarks. Most adopted the name Trinity House, and Trinity House of Deptford Strond became influential and powerful when it received its charter from Henry VIII in 1515, assuming general powers to order the safety of shipping and the welfare of seamen and their dependents.

An act of parliament of 1566 described Trinity House of Deptford Strond as navigational experts, empowered to erect beacons, marks and signs for navigation on headlands, shores and forelands at their expense and when necessary, and this was extended thirty years later to cover the positioning of buoys.

Trinity House claimed the exclusive right to erect lighthouses — as opposed to beacons, marks, and signs — but parliament retained this lucrative right for the Crown; it incorporated the power to levy dues. Advantage was taken by the Crown, which granted patents to favourites and other private individuals, and many speculators made fortunes from their lighthouses (and as many ruined themselves), a proportion of the profits going to the royal exchequer.

15

Lighthouses were haphazardly maintained and Trinity House took little interest in their actual construction, usually leasing their patent to a private person or company, at least up to the 1780s. They were rarely the first to suggest the construction of a lighthouse and often opposed petitions on the grounds that, had a light been necessary, they themselves would have suggested it. Another popular argument was that the illumination of Britain's coasts was tantamount to guiding the enemy fleets. The need for acceptable national standards was being felt increasingly, however, and after 1785 Trinity House answered criticisms of the way in which privately owned lights were run by starting to look closely at their operation. The original patents were expiring in many cases, and as this happened Trinity House began to assume a much fuller control than previously and to take upon itself the responsibilities which it bears today.

Trinity House coat of arms c1670

Annual profits of about £20,000 were reached at the turn of the eighteenth century and were used to benefit their charities — Trinity House was a semi-religious organisation and owned a hall and almshouses at Deptford. In 1836, when Trinity House was empowered to control all English lights, compensation of £1,200,000 was paid with the aid of a government grant to private owners.

Modern Trinity House maintains over ninety lighthouses, nearly thirty lightships and about 700 buoys, and regularly inspects seamarks maintained by local authorities within the limits of their home ports. Its policy is one of continuous experimentation and improvement in the areas of construction, power generation, light and fog signal efficiency, and many lighthouses are being equipped with a new apparatus. It was instrumental in the development of RACON, the radar beacon which strengthens the display on a ship's radar screen to indicate the bearing of the lighthouse or lightship, and LANBY, the large automatic navigation buoy which is replacing a number of lightships.

Safety at sea is a cause which demands complete efficiency and a working knowledge of all the circumstances in which a ship may find herself, which is why Trinity House has maintained a tradition of administration by a board of master mariners. It is the lighthouse authority for England, Wales, the Channel Islands with adjacent seas and islands, and Gibraltar, and as a charitable organisation it controls trusts dedicated to the relief of aged master mariners, their widows and unmarried daughters.

Lighthouse Illumination

Early Lights
The earliest coastal lights were coal fires raised on towers, and many tons of coal were transported to fuel lights such as the one built at Tynemouth in 1550. Keepers at Spurn Head regularly complained of the difficulty of dragging coal carts over the sand and shingle. Life for keepers must have been hard, particularly on nights of strong wind when a fire would consume tons of coal in

Dungeness lighthouse c1690

a single night and the fire would burn so fiercely that its cresset or iron grate would melt. At other times, it would prove impossible to maintain a steady bright light, and when it was wet and stormy the light would be shrouded in smoke. Lanterns were built to enclose the fires, but smoke soon blackened the glass, an example of this fault being recorded in 1680 at St Agnes lighthouse in the Scilly Isles.

Mariners had difficulty in distinguishing between one coal-fired light and another and attempts were made to overcome this by using multiple lights: three at the Casquets and four at the Lizard, for example. Coal fires were still in operation at St Bees and Flatholm as late as 1822.

Candles and oil

Candles were used in many early lights but though capable of producing a constant glow their power was small. They were often grouped, as in the Eddystone lighthouse in 1759 which had a two-ring candelabrum holding twenty-four candles. The wicks had to be snuffed regularly and the keepers were reminded of this task by a clock that struck every thirty minutes. Early oil lamps gave off a great deal of smoke and needed regular attention if they were not to soot up the glass; the flat-wicked lamps were fuelled initially with sperm oil and later with vegetable oil.

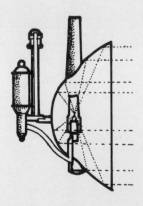

Argand burner and parabolic reflector

Vaporised oil lamps

In 1782, Aimé Argand invented the burner that still bears his name; it used a circular wick with a central draught of air, and with a surrounding glass chimney gave a brilliant, smokeless and steady flame. With later improvements by Thomas Stevenson, Douglass and Fresnel the Argand burner remained the principal source of lighthouse illumination for the next century. The Kitson vaporised oil burner of 1901 provided a light three times more powerful than that of the Argand lamp, and an improved and simplified version became standard equipment in our lighthouses in the 1920s and is still in use in some today.

Reflectors

Without a means of projection, light wastes most of its intensity through diffusion; with a reflector, it can be directed. The benefit of the parabolic reflector, its ability to direct an accurate beam of light, was discovered in the middle of the eighteenth century by William Hutchinson who built several of small squares of mirrored glass set in plaster of Paris. Some of the Liverpool lighthouses were fitted, and Walney lighthouse had a 36in reflector with 721 facets. The glass reflectors were extremely heavy and were later replaced by hand-beaten silver and copper; in conjunction with the Argand lamp, they were standard equipment in most Trinity House stations by 1800. The largest reflector, 13½ft in diameter, was installed at Bidston Hill lighthouse but the normal diameter was in the region of 21in; it was calculated that a reflector used with a fixed optic increased light intensity 350 times and with a revolving optic 450 times.

The potential of giving a light a definite characteristic by arranging the reflectors in a certain way was studied, and it was found possible to produce group flashing, ie two or three flashes followed by a period of darkness. Robert Stevenson installed such a system at Walney in 1820; it comprised four Argands and reflectors on a revolving frame.

The dioptric lens

The most important development in illumination was introduced in 1822 when Augustin Fresnel invented his refracting or dioptric lens. He used a bull's-eye lens surrounded by concentric rings of prismatic glass, each ring projecting a little beyond the previous one, the effect being to refract or bend into a horizontal beam most of the light from the source. The rings were known as dioptrics. Further reflecting prisms, called catadioptrics, were added above and below the rings to collect upward and downward rays which might otherwise have escaped. Many improvements were made by Thomas Stevenson and James Timmins Chance but the system is essentially the same today. Sometimes two lenses were used, one above the other, with a burner at the centre of each; these were known as biform optics, and the type was introduced at the Eddystone and Bishop Rock.

The interest in lighthouse illumination was such that in 1850 Chance Brothers of Smethwick set up a full-time lighthouse optical department at their glassworks.

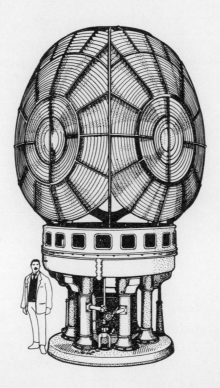

Hyperradial optic: one of the largest optics ever built

Lighthouse optics are classified according to the focal length of the centre lens:

Hyperradial	1,330mm focal length
1st order	920mm
2nd order	700mm
3rd order	500mm
3rd order small	375mm
4th order	250mm
5th order	187.5mm
6th order	150mm

The 3rd order small optic has a high efficiency and is in use in many places throughout the world; the enormous hyperradial, developed in 1885, was installed in only a few lighthouses. Many of the larger optics are now being replaced by smaller units, a move which great increases in light intensity has made possible.

Electricity

The first experiments with electricity took place at Dungeness in 1862, but the system was not widely adopted because of its expense. Further experiments were made at South Foreland, St Catherine's and the Lizard, this time with cored carbons in arc lamps, but although powerful the lamps were unsatisfactory because the flame of the arcs was difficult to control, resulting in a haphazard light. They were replaced with high-power filament lamps when electricity from the main grid became available. Most lighthouses are now electrified, including many rock stations, where generators and banks of batteries have been installed.

A xenon arc lamp, recently tested at Dungeness, gave a light of extremely high intensity which, like its predecessor 100 years before, proved difficult to control and was abandoned as unsuccessful.

Gas

When the incandescent mantle was invented, the revolution in domestic lighting was extended into lighthouse illumination. Early attempts to oust coal fires by coal gas were made by Trinity House in 1780, but were abandoned until, thirty years later, the threat of a shortage of sperm oil promoted further tests. Meanwhile, experi-

22

ments which involved the burning of hydrogen in air were made and abandoned.

Lack of success attended Sir Goldsworthy Gurney's manipulation of Argand lamps at Bude and Lt Thomas Drummond's limelight, produced by the combustion of oxygen and hydrogen on a bed of lime, tested at South Foreland in 1862.

Three years later, coal gas produced on-site was used to power the light at Happisburgh, Norfolk, and was in use even earlier at Hartlepool, but the drawback to coal gas was the need for plentiful supplies of coal which, though available, could not easily be taken to many lighthouses and not at all to others. Engineers accepted this limitation and turned their attention to the perfection of other sources of power. David and Charles Stevenson developed the use of acetylene dissolved in acetone and stored under great pressure in a cylinder. This allowed automatic lighting and was installed in many unwatched stations around the Scottish coast; it could be adapted to power explosive fog warning guns.

Today, most unwatched lighthouses and most buoys use this system; light-sensitive switches control the gas supply.

Solar and wind energy

At Crossness lighthouse, an unmanned Thames station, the light is powered by energy from the sun, converted into electricity by solar cells and stored in batteries. Power supply is controlled by a light-sensitive switch and energy stored during the summer months is sufficient to maintain the light during the winter.

The British Isles are among the windiest of the world's developed countries, and the wind-power potential is enormous. The Trinity House research and development team installed a wind generator on a 30ft tower at Dungeness experimental station with encouraging results, and the generator is intended ultimately for Godrevy Island in Cornwall. Trinity House hope to install others.

LIGHT CHARACTERISTICS

Each light has a distinctive characteristic which enables ships' masters to recognise and identify it positively. No light is placed close to another with a similar characteristic and in the case of landfall lights no light within 100 miles has a potentially confusing appearance. Landfall lights are normally equipped with the most powerful apparatus — 1st order optics — and are usually flashing in characteristic.

Characteristics fall into three groups:

Fixed Lights which are shown without interruption, ie which do not flash.

Rhythmic Lights which show a sequence of light and darkness, repeated identically at regular intervals. The time taken to show one complete sequence is known as the period of the light.

Alternating Rhythmic lights which exhibit different colours during each sequence. The period of an alternating light is the time taken to exhibit the complete sequence, including all colour changes.

Within the last two groups, a large number of distinctive combinations can be formed by varying periods of light and darkness and different colours; the basic categories are:

Flashing and *quick flashing*
Isophase (equal periods of light and darkness)
Occulting (longer periods of light, shorter of darkness)
Morse code (long and short flashes to represent letters in the morse code alphabet)

Combinations such as *alternating fixed and flashing* and *group flashing* (a number of flashes in a group, repeated regularly) enable each light to have a virtually unique characteristic.

Some lighthouse optics revolve to give a flashing characteristic, showing a light or combination of lights at each revolution. Clockwork mechanisms, once common, are still in use at a few stations; they were hand-wound or powered by weights (like a grandfather clock) in deep shafts or hanging down cliff faces. Small electric motors are more usual today.

Optics are heavy, in some cases reaching several tons, and smooth revolution is achieved by floating them on a bath of mercury; they will move at the touch of a finger. Alternatively, they rotate on a bed of rollers (a roller carriage) or a ball bearing column.

Fog Signals

The introduction of fog signals is of comparatively recent date; gongs and bells were used initially, but there was an almost complete lack of fog warning at coastal stations until the middle of the nineteenth century. Douglass's Eddystone lighthouse was fitted with two 2-ton bells, but even these were inaudible at a distance of a few hundred yards.

Guns were used at many land stations and on lightships, and sound rockets (maroons) charged with guncotton were in use in 1878 at Flamborough Head. At most rock stations, bells were replaced by explosive signals suspended from an iron jib projecting from the lantern and consisting usually of 4oz charges fired by a detonator connected to an electric battery. Stevenson's fog gun, in which a mixture of acetylene and air was exploded at intervals in a firing chamber, replaced many of the manually-operated devices.

Fog signal emitters fall into the following broad categories:

Diaphone This is powered by compressed air and generally emits a powerful, low-pitched sound which often ends with a brief lowering of pitch to produce a 'grunt'. The operating machinery comprises compressed-air generators and air-storage facilities, and may be housed in custom-built quarters or on the ground floor of the tower.

Horn Compressed air or electricity vibrates a diaphragm to produce a range of sounds from powerful multiple-emitter blasts at major stations to single steady tones at harbour entrances and approaches.

Siren A compressed-air device, considered (with the diaphone) until recently to be among the most efficient emitters.

Reed Another compressed-air instrument, sometimes hand-operated, which gives out a weak high-pitched sound.

Explosive Short reports are produced by the firing of explosive charges.

Bell, gong, whistle   If sounded mechanically, these produce a regular sound effective over a short distance; if operated by hand or wave action, the sound is erratic.

The *supertyfon*, a powerful horn unit, is usually installed in groups, a similarity it shares with the *tannoy*. This is loudspeaker-like in operation, electrically powered, and usually assembled in banks of precast concrete horns.

The powerful nautophone, developed in 1929 and installed at some Trinity House stations, produces a high-pitch, high-intensity note from an electrically-vibrated diaphragm. Compact electric fog signals are being built, or are already in use, at many land stations today. Sixty emitters were built into the tower of the new lighthouse at Dungeness in 1961 and a similar architectural feature encloses a bank of emitters at Tater-du, one of the most recently commissioned English lights (1965). Experimental work with automatic fog detector/warnings is being carried out at isolated unmanned rock stations.

The *Admiralty List of Lights and Fog Signals* warns seamen that fog signals are heard over distances which vary greatly, and that there may be areas around a station where the signal is totally

Diaphone fog signal house, Bull Point (destroyed by coastal erosion 1972)

Tannoy electric fog signal, St Ann's Head

inaudible. Under some atmospheric conditions, certain tones —
perhaps the high tones — of multiple-tone emitters may not be
heard.

Sounds representing letters of the morse code are given out by
some stations, and others produce a tone which varies continually
— the warble tone.

MAP A

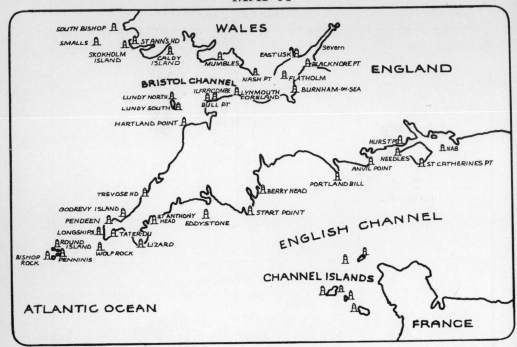

WALES

SOUTH BISHOP

SMALLS

SKOKHOLM ISLAND   ST ANN'S HD

CALDY ISLAND

EAST USK   Severn

MUMBLES   BLACKNORE PT

NASH PT   ENGLAND

BRISTOL CHANNEL   FLATHOLM

ILFRACOMBE   BURNHAM-ON-SEA

LUNDY NORTH   LYNMOUTH FORELAND

LUNDY SOUTH   BULL PT

HARTLAND POINT

HURST PT

NEEDLES   NAB

ANVIL POINT   ST CATHERINES PT

PORTLAND BILL

TREVOSE HD   BERRY HEAD

GODREVY ISLAND   START POINT

PENDEEN   ST ANTHONY HEAD   EDDYSTONE

LONGSHIPS   TATER-DU   ENGLISH CHANNEL

ROUND ISLAND   LIZARD

BISHOP ROCK   WOLF ROCK

PENNINIS   CHANNEL ISLANDS

ATLANTIC OCEAN   FRANCE

MAP B

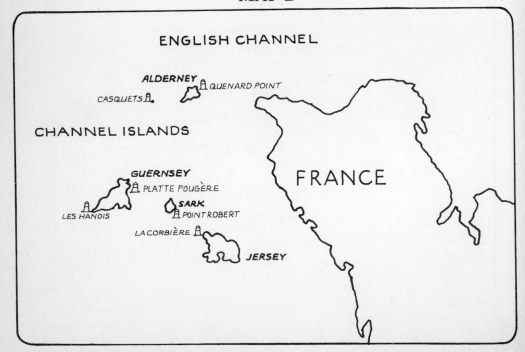

ENGLISH CHANNEL

ALDERNEY   QUENARD POINT

CASQUETS

CHANNEL ISLANDS

FRANCE

GUERNSEY   PLATTE FOUGÈRE

LES HANOIS   SARK

POINT ROBERT

LA CORBIÈRE

JERSEY

MAP C

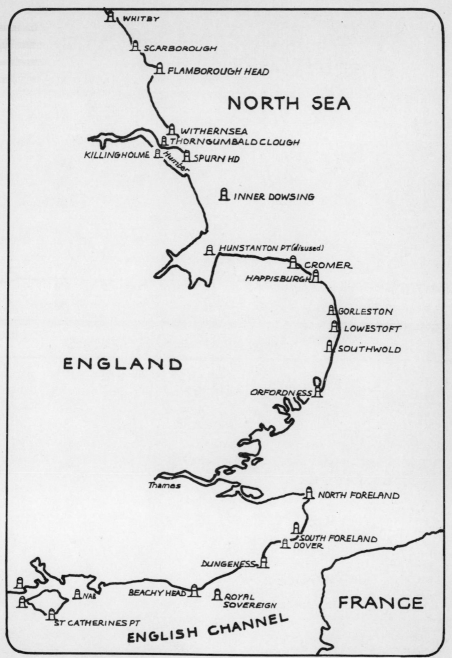

WHITBY

SCARBOROUGH

FLAMBOROUGH HEAD

NORTH SEA

WITHERNSEA
THORNGUMBALD CLOUGH
KILLINGHOLME — Humber — SPURN HD

INNER DOWSING

HUNSTANTON PT (disused)
CROMER
HAPPISBURGH

GORLESTON
LOWESTOFT
SOUTHWOLD

ENGLAND

ORFORDNESS

Thames

NORTH FORELAND

SOUTH FORELAND
DOVER

DUNGENESS

NAB
BEACHY HEAD
ROYAL SOVEREIGN

FRANCE

ST CATHERINES PT

ENGLISH CHANNEL

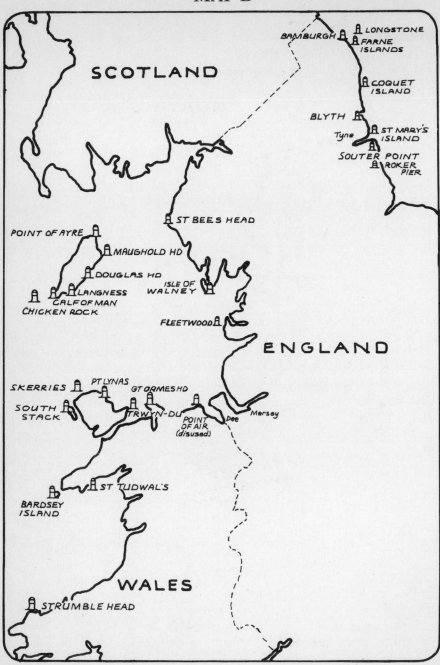

SCOTLAND

BAMBURGH
LONGSTONE
FARNE
ISLANDS

COQUET
ISLAND

BLYTH
ST MARY'S
ISLAND
Tyne
SOUTER POINT
ROKER
PIER

ST BEES HEAD

POINT OF AYRE
MAUGHOLD HD
DOUGLAS HD
ISLE OF
WALNEY
LANGNESS
CALF OF MAN
CHICKEN ROCK

FLEETWOOD

ENGLAND

SKERRIES
PT LYNAS
GT ORMES HD
SOUTH
STACK
TRWYN-DU
POINT
OF AIR
(disused)
Dee
Mersey

BARDSEY
ISLAND
ST TUDWAL'S

WALES

STRUMBLE HEAD

KEY TO ABBREVIATIONS

MHW	*mean high water*
F	*fixed (light)*
Fl	*flashing*
Gp Fl	*group flashing*
QFl	*quick flashing*
Iso	*isophase*
Alt	*alternating*
Occ	*occulting*
Mo	*morse code*
cp	*candlepower*
G	*green*
R	*red*
W	*white*
Range	*ie in clear weather*
(-sec)	*the period of the light*
	the interval between fog signal sounds or groups of sounds

See Light Characteristics (page 23) for explanations of alternating isophase and occulting.

The date given for the establishment of a lighthouse station indicates the first involvement of an authority such as Trinity House; the text supplements this information with references to earlier known lights. Dates of present towers are given only where different from the dates of establishment.

THE SOUTH COAST

Bishop Rock to Nab Tower (Map A p 28)

Beachy Head to North Foreland (Map C p 29)

BISHOP ROCK

James Walker, engineer to Trinity House, decided against a solid
granite lighthouse for this station, arguing that the rock ledge,
barely 153ft long by 52ft wide and rising sheer from a depth of
150ft, was too small, and the elements too powerful, exposed as
it was to the full force of the Atlantic Ocean. He showed that wind
pressures at times exceeded 7,000lb/sq ft, and as many as thirty
gales in one year were not unusual in that area. Thus it was decided
in 1847 to erect a screw-pile lighthouse on the Bishop Rock at a
cost of £12,000. The first task was to sink cast iron legs into the
solid granite, braced and stayed with wrought iron rods. The
designer maintained that the waves would be able to roll freely

Cross section of Original Lighthouse

Bishop Rock: one of the world's most exposed stations

35

among the piles instead of being obstructed by the solid mass of a masonry tower. When work was suspended at the end of 1849 the building was complete except for the installation of the lighting apparatus, but before it could be finished the following season a heavy gale swept away the whole structure on the evening of 5 February 1850.

Undismayed by the failure of the first lighthouse, James Walker once again turned to the idea of a granite tower based upon Smeaton's Eddystone. After surveying the site, he finally chose a small but solid mass giving him room for a base 35ft in diameter. The surface of the rock was to be trimmed to receive the foundation courses, but the waves constantly swept over the site and the lowest blocks had to be laid 1ft below low water mark. A heavy cofferdam was erected around the site and the water pumped out so that the masons could work on a dry rock face. Each granite block, weighing from one to two tons, was set into its preselected position, and each course was dovetailed and keyed at the sides, top and bottom, forming an immovable mass.

The workmen were housed on a small uninhabited islet nearby where living quarters and workshops were erected, and carried to and from the site as the weather permitted. Working spells were brief, as well as being few and far between, but after seven years' work the tower was completed. All the granite was dispatched from the mainland to the island depot where it was shaped and numbered before being sent to the rock. In all, the tower contained 2,500 tons of dressed granite, and cost £34,560. The foundation stone was laid on 16 July 1852 and the light was first exhibited on 1 September 1858. Four keepers were appointed to watch over the powerful light, three on station at the rock and the fourth on leave at St Mary's. During one particularly bad storm, waves rolled up the side of the lighthouse and tore the 550lb fog bell from its fastening on the lantern gallery.

In 1881, Sir James Douglass made a detailed inspection of the tower and reported extensive damage and weakness in the structure. It was decided to strengthen the tower and at the same time to increase the elevation of the light by 40ft. The plans, complex in nature, essentially entailed the building of a new lighthouse around the old one, completely encasing it. The real weakness was the foundation, which Douglass proposed to strengthen and enlarge with massive blocks of granite sunk into the rock and held by heavy bolts. It was an enormous cylindrical base, providing the lighthouse with an excellent buffer on which the force of the waves could be spent before they hit the tower. The masonry casing was carried up to the point where the new extension began, and the work was completed in 1887 at a cost of £66,000, nearly 6,000 tons of granite being used.

The 11-ton lens originally revolved on rollers but now turns at the touch of a finger on its mercury bath.

Bishop Rock is included in the list of lighthouses due for modernisation, with possible conversion to electricity and the building of a helicopter platform.

Two disasters of note occurred a short way off the Bishop Rock, the first in 1707 when a British squadron missed the St Agnes light in a gale and all but two frigates were blown on to the Gilstone Rock. More than 1,800 men were drowned, and although Admiral Sir Cloudesley Shovel is said to have reached the shore alive he also perished. Three hundred people were lost when the German steam packet *Schiller* drove on to the Retarrier Rocks in 1875.

Established 1858 (present tower 1887)
Height of light above MHW 143ft
Height of tower 167ft
Range 29 miles
W Gp Fl (15sec), 720,000cp
Hyperradial biform optic
Electricity, 240V 1500W
Supertyfon fog horns (90sec) 2 blasts
No public access

PENINNIS HEAD

A patent of June 1680 authorised Trinity House to build a lighthouse on St Agnes and to levy tolls for its support, provided the dues were 'reasonable' and the profits devoted to its charities.

The surveyors, Capt Hugh Tiel and Capt Simon Bayley, encountered opposition from the inhabitants, who derived benefits from shipwreck, but plans were drawn and permission given by the government for the purchase of materials from the naval stores at Plymouth.

St Agnes old lighthouse: now a popular tourist attraction, this disused lighthouse marks the site of one of the earliest British coastal beacons

The lighthouse was to be four storeys high with walls 6ft thick at the base, and all timber was to be 'of the best English heart oak'. The light, a fire of coals in a glass lantern with ventilation funnels, was 200ft above high water. It was kindled on 30 October 1680, and the cost was found to have been so great that Trinity House, impoverished, asked the master, the Duke of York, to forgo his salary.

The lantern sooted up quickly and needed constant cleaning, and in 1740 the keepers were accused by Trinity House of inordinate drinking and failing to keep the light in an effective condition.

Fifty years later, modernisation was carried out, and an oil light with parabolic reflectors was installed. The tower continued in service until 1911, when it was replaced by an automatic light on Peninnis Head.

> Present tower (Peninnis) built 1911
> Height of light above MHW 110ft
> Height of tower 45ft
> Range 16.4 miles
> W Fl (15sec), 100,000cp
> Optic 3rd order catadioptric
> Acetylene
> No public access (unwatched)

St Agnes old lighthouse grate: this cast iron grate burned up to 107 tons of coal a year; it is preserved in the Tresco Gardens

ROUND ISLAND

Round Island is the most northerly outpost of the Scillies. A lightship is moored between it and the mainland near the Seven Stones Rocks on which, in 1966, the 61,000-ton oil tanker *Torrey Canyon* was wrecked and broke into three parts, spilling millions of gallons of oil and creating a state of emergency for Cornish seaside communities and disaster for marine life.

Round Island is a 130ft mass of granite, the top forming a platform on which Trinity House built a lighthouse and dwellings in 1887 under conditions of extreme difficulty. The sheer rock face made the off-loading of building materials almost impossible, and the only access today (apart from the regular relief helicopter) is by a flight of steps cut into the solid rock.

The enormous hyperradial optic, fitted to only two other lighthouses at the beginning of the twentieth century, was replaced in 1967 with modern apparatus.

Established 1887
Height of light above MHW 180ft
Height of tower 63ft
Range 19.7 miles

39

Round Island: a lonely station guarding the western approaches to the Scilly Isles

R Fl (10sec), 460,000cp
Sealed beam units (20)
Electricity, 30V 200W
Fog siren (60sec) 4 blasts
No public access

LONGSHIPS

The cliffs and rocks of Land's End have always been a threat to shipping, and many vessels caught in an Atlantic gale have been wrecked here in sight of home. Of the many rocks, the Carn Bras is the most dangerous; this group lies about a mile westward from Land's End and rises to 50ft. In bad weather, it is a battleground of sea and wind, and landing is made difficult by surf even on moderately calm days. Dense fogbanks form quickly in all weathers.

Lieutenant Henry Smith was granted a lease in 1795 to build a lighthouse on the Longships, four years after Trinity House obtained a patent but abandoned the project as impracticable. The three-storey circular tower of granite, designed by Samuel Wyatt for Smith, was built without delay and the Argand burners first lit in 1795. Smith went bankrupt soon afterwards and Trinity House took over the lease, which they finally bought for about £40,000 in 1836.

Four keepers were appointed, each earning £30 per year and receiving free food when on duty. Life was hard for them, and was not made easier by a feature of the station: the rush of wind through a fissure and past a cavern produced such a noise that sleep was often impossible. One keeper was so terrified, it is claimed, that his hair turned white and he lost his senses. Another keeper, cautioned against fooling about on the rock, fell over the side to his death. Many other stories are told about this station, but most are fiction (see *Watchers on the Longships* by James F. Cobb).

The light was so often eclipsed by the sea washing over the lantern that Sir James Douglass, the chief engineer of Trinity House, was called in to design a much higher light, which was built on the principles of Smeaton's Eddystone and is still in service today, having been modernised in 1967. In spite of the increase in height, the lantern panes are reached by spray on stormy days.

Today, as at all rock stations, two sets of three keepers alternate one month of duty with one month ashore. A novel signal arrangement has been introduced by the keepers and their wives a mile away at Sennen Cove. At 2pm each day, news is exchanged by semaphore flags.

Longships is included in the helicopter relief schedule.

Longships: the present tower

Established 1795 (present tower 1883)
Height of light above MHW 114ft
Height of tower 117ft
Range 17.4 miles
W R Iso (10sec), 72,000cp
Optic 1st order dioptric
Electricity, 240V 1,500W
Supertyfon fog horns (15sec)
No public access

WOLF ROCK

Wolf Rock owes its name to the wolf-like wail of air escaping from a hollow where it was compressed by incoming waves. The sound was so pronounced that shipping could set a course by it, but local people filled the fissure with stones and silenced the sound.

Trinity House rejected a proposal for a bell buoy in 1750, backed by fishermen who feared that it would frighten the fish, and when a lighthouse was considered by Lieut Henry Smith in 1791 he concluded that the task was beyond him. Instead of a lighthouse, he offered to set up a 20ft iron mast with a wolf's-head

Wolf Rock: built on a 170ft x 100ft rock platform twenty miles out to sea

figure at the top, jaws open, to recreate by wind action the sound of the wolf. The mast was built, but even though it was only 4in in diameter and well-stayed it was soon washed away.

In 1835 James Walker, engineer to Trinity House, built a structure of solid concrete encased in iron plates. The base was 16ft in diameter and although the tower was only 16ft in height it took five seasons to complete. John Thorburn took charge of the operations and the final cost was £11,298.

The present lighthouse was designed by James Walker and built by Nicholas Douglass, father of Sir James. After surveying the site for a foundation the engineer was in danger of being marooned on the rock because the boat could not approach. He saved himself by tying a lifeline round his waist and jumping into the sea to be dragged into the waiting boat.

A feature of the Wolf is the substantial landing stage adjoining the tower. It was necessary to construct this platform before the lighthouse could be built. Once completed, a derrick was erected and the large dressed granite blocks were unloaded from the supply ship. Work went slowly for two seasons, as each dovetailed block was anchored in place and held with cement and clamps, and only thirty-seven blocks were set. The structural work was not completed for five years more; nearly 300 landings were made on the rock, and the final cost was £62,726, about £30,000 below the estimate of Robert Stevenson, chief engineer to the Northern Lighthouse Board and builder of the Bell Rock lighthouse in Scotland.

Tragedy struck on 18 December 1969 when one of the keepers fell to his death. He was last seen fishing from the winch room and his body was never found. The coroner recorded an open verdict.

During 1973, Trinity House erected a large cage-like structure over the lantern. This is an experimental helicopter landing platform, which could be the prototype for other such structures on waveswept towers. The first successful helicopter relief of the Wolf Rock took place on 3 November 1973, although the helicopter did not land.

Established 1870
Height of light above MHW 110ft
Height of tower 135ft

Range 16.4 miles
W R Alt Fl (30sec), 378,000cp
Optic 4th order catadioptric
Electricity, 100V 1,000W
Diaphone fog signal (30sec)
No public access

TATER-DU

The coastline from Hartland Point round to the Lizard is one of
high rugged cliffs, often over 200ft above sea level, with rocks
lying beneath the sea and stretching out into dangerous reefs. From
Trevose Head, shipping rounding the point picks up the lights of
Pendeen, Longships, Wolf Rock and Lizard but the need was felt
for a landward light between Longships and the Lizard, reinforced

Tater-du: built in 1965 to complete the lighting of the tip of Cornwall

by the wrecking on 3 November 1962 of a French trawler bound for Dieppe from the Irish Coast. Six lives were saved, two by helicopter and four by breeches buoy. As an extra aid to shipping Trinity House planned Tater-du, positioning this new lighthouse between Lamorna and Porthcurno.

The station, which was opened by HRH the Duke of Gloucester, former Master of Trinity House, in 1965, can be reached by a difficult cliff walk from Lamorna Cove.

Established 1965
Height of light above MHW 112ft
Height of tower 50ft
Range 16.5 miles
W Gp Fl (15sec), 300,000cp
Optic 4th order catadioptric
Electricity, 50V 250W
Tannoy fog horns (30sec) 2 blasts
No public access (unwatched)

THE LIZARD

Much exaggerated nonsense has been written about the activities of wreckers, but small communities undoubtedly and often officially derived benefit from the spoils of shipwreck. There was sometimes objection, therefore, when lighthouses were proposed, and petitions were occasionally rejected on the strength of local feeling; this was true particularly of the south west of England.

The Lizard Point in Cornwall, where as early as 1570 a light was considered necessary, was the scene of local opposition which was overcome eventually by Sir John Killigrew, a philanthropic Cornishman who obtained from James I a patent to erect a lighthouse at his own expense for a rent of 'twenty nobles by the year' for a term of thirty years. Moreover, he could collect from ships that passed the point any voluntary contributions that the owners might offer him. He needed these contributions to purchase fuel for the fires, for although he was willing to build the tower he was too poor to bear alone the cost of maintenance. The king's council considered the request and passed it to Trinity House for their comments. The king was advised not to grant the patent because it

Lizard: the present station; the original lighthouse (1752) had four towers and consumed a huge quantity of coal each night

was thought a light on Lizard Point would guide enemy vessels and pirates to a safe landing. Killigrew was not without influential friends, however, and with the support of his cousin Lord Dorchester, and Lord Buckingham, was granted the patent he required with one proviso: that the light should be extinguished at the approach of the enemy.

Within a few months, work was under way and it was hoped to finish the tower by September 1619 and have it lit before the storms of the autumn. Killigrew found it almost impossible to recruit local labour, but by Christmas 1619 was ready to kindle the light. The cost of the tower, which was built of stone and lime, amounted to £500; this, together with maintenance of about ten shillings a night, drastically cut into his diminishing funds. It was a superb light for those days, and shipowners reaped the benefit but offered nothing for its upkeep. Killigrew approached the king, requesting a compulsory levy to be made on shipping, and in the face of opposition from Trinity House James I set a fee of one halfpenny a ton on all vessels passing the light. This caused such an uproar from the shipowners that the patent was withdrawn, the light extinguished and the tower demolished.

46

Although applications were made in ensuing years, it was not until 1748 that Trinity House supported an attempt by Thomas Fonnerau to erect a lighthouse. He proposed to build four towers, offering Trinity House a rent of £80 a year for a lease of sixty-one years. The four towers, each over 40ft in height and fitted with glass lanterns, were completed in 1751 at a cost of £3,000 and the coal fires were kindled. Complaints were made about their dimness, but nothing was done to improve them. The patent expired, and in 1812 Trinity House made structural alterations, leaving the station much as it is today.

Established 1751
Height of light above MHW 230ft
Height of tower 61ft
Range 21.8 miles
W Fl (3sec), 4,000,000cp
Optic 2nd order catadioptric
Electricity, 100V 300W
Fog siren (60sec) Mo(N)
Open to public

ST ANTHONY HEAD

The beautiful headlands of the eastern and western sides of the entrance to Falmouth Harbour have seen many fascinating aspects of naval history. The towering slopes rise to 250ft and are covered in woodlands. Today some of the trees have gone, but Pendennis Castle, built by Henry VIII, and survivor of a siege in 1645, still stands on the western shore. With the castle at St Mawes on the opposite side it completed the defences of this magnificent natural harbour. The waters of Falmouth Bay and Carrick Roads now abound in private yachts and motor boats, and it is by boat that the splendour of the rivers and branching creeks of the Fal estuary are best appreciated.

Trinity House built the lighthouse at the eastern side of the harbour, a fine station designed by their chief engineer, James Walker. It stands on a bluff at the foot of the headland, and in order to make a firm and level foundation for the tower and buildings a walled granite platform was first constructed, on which James Walker planned to build the eight-sided tower.

St Anthony Head: a 2 ton fog bell once hung from a bracket beneath the lantern gallery

Two lights were originally exhibited, one of them to guide ships past the Manacles Rocks, and a 2-ton fog bell hanging from a bracket beneath the lantern was struck every minute. The lower light and bell were abandoned when the station was modernised in 1911.

Established 1835
Height of light above MHW 72ft
Height of tower 62ft
Range 14 miles
W R Occ (20sec), 225,000cp
Optic 1st order catadioptric
Electricity, 100V 2,250W
Nautophone fog signal (20sec)
Open to public

EDDYSTONE

The Eddystone Rock, which lies about 14 miles SSW of Plymouth, in the centre of the busy sea-route of the English Channel, was the scene of so many shipwrecks in Stuart times that a decision was taken to erect a permanent lighthouse. The difficulties at first

Eddystone: the five lighthouses (from left to right) — 1698, 1699,1709, 1759, 1882

seemed insurmountable because the reef was above water only at low tide and the sea was often rough. Furthermore, such a lighthouse had never been built before so there was no example to work from.

Henry Winstanley's light

Henry Winstanley, an eccentric of Littlebury in Essex, obtained a patent and undertook to design and build a lighthouse on the Eddystone Rock. Work began in 1696 when twelve holes were bored in the rock and iron rods secured in them with lead. In the second season a solid circular pillar 12ft high and 14ft in diameter was built to encase the rods. This base was increased in diameter by 2ft the following year and the tower of wood and stone was erected to a height of 80ft above the rock. The lantern was first lighted on 14 November 1698. Winstanley realised that the tower was too small when he saw the winter gales sweep right over it, and in 1699 the whole superstructure was removed and the base further extended to 24ft in diameter. The new tower took on a fantastic appearance as it rose to 100ft. Built of stone and wood, it looked

49

like a Chinese pagoda surmounted by a lantern gallery and heavily ornamented with wrought iron. The total cost to Winstanley was £8,000, and he had the greatest confidence in his work, going so far as to express a desire to be at the lighthouse during a gale, and in November 1703 went out with a repair gang. On the evening of 26 November what came to be called the 'great storm' sprang up, and when dawn broke nothing remained of men or lighthouse.

However critical people may have been of Winstanley's elaborate pagoda, it must be remembered that he was the first engineer to attempt to build a rock lighthouse. He had no precedent, and he proved that it could be done. The main faults of the design lay in the lack of weight and the inadequate way in which the base was fixed to the reef. The 'great storm' was said to have been the worst in recorded history. In London, £1 million-worth of damage was done; in Kent, 17,000 trees were uprooted and church steeples were toppled.

John Rudyerd's light

Shortly after the loss of Winstanley's light, the *Winchelsea*, homeward bound from America, was wrecked on the Eddystone with appalling loss of life. The value of a lighthouse at this place was again emphasised but Trinity House still refused to accept responsibility for building one. Captain John Lovett obtained a patent and leased the rock for 99 years, and by act of parliament was permitted to collect a toll of 1d per ton from all ships passing the light. He commissioned John Rudyerd, a silk mercer of Ludgate Hill, to design and build the tower and Rudyerd at once enlisted the help of two shipwrights, Smith and Norcutt of the naval dockyard at Woolwich.

The construction was a skilful piece of nautical engineering: a smooth shape, free of projections and clad in planks of ships' timber. A base was built of sixteen layers of stone separated by timber, all jointed and keyed together to form a solid mass 23ft in height. To hold the tower to the rock, thirty-six holes were bored with special dovetailed sections into which large bolts were set, wedged and sealed with red-hot pewter. The wooden tower was raised to 69ft, a height above the sea of 92ft. The interior was divided into four rooms, the uppermost of which rose an octagonal lantern crowned with a ball. The building was completed in 1709.

It was attacked by seaworms that ate into the wood, and several of the exterior cladding timbers were replaced, but the lighthouse stood firmly for fifty years until 2 December 1755 when one of the keepers went up to trim the candles and found the lantern full of smoke. It burst into flames when he opened the door. The three keepers tried desperately to put out the fire, but at length, driven back by the smoke, they sought safety in a cave among the rocks. They were rescued, but one of them, Henry Hall, died twelve days afterwards. He claimed he had swallowed some molten lead. He was not believed, but a doctor removed from his stomach a flat oval-shaped lump of lead weighing 7oz which is still preserved today in the Edinburgh Museum.

John Smeaton's light

To maintain a light on the Eddystone reef, Trinity House stationed a lightship there as a temporary measure. John Smeaton, recommended by the Royal Society, was asked to design and build a new lighthouse. He studied the plans of the previous towers and, influenced to some extent by the shape of old oaks round his home, planned a lighthouse with a broad base and curving sides. He proposed to build it entirely of stone, much to the horror of his critics who said that only a wooden structure had enough flexibility to withstand the force of the waves. Smeaton countered by suggesting that it was the weight of 500 tons of stone that kept Rudyerd's tower on the rock, not the timber.

In August 1756 work began on the foundation. The upper surface of the rock was carefully removed and steps were accurately cut and dovetailed ready for the first blocks, due to be shipped out the following season. During the winter, masons cut and shaped the blocks while Smeaton experimented with quick-drying waterproof cements. The granite blocks delivered from Dartmoor and Exmoor were cut and shaped with dovetails that fitted exactly, so that each course was a solid mass. They were numbered and a model made of each one so that should any be lost they could be recut. As each course was completed, it was laid out in the yard as it would be on the rock. The next course was then laid on top and holes were bored through each stone to receive trenails of very hard oak, which when driven through would fix the stone to the one below it, holding them firmly until the cement had set. As the

courses were built up, wedges were driven into grooves cut vertically down the edges of adjoining stones. Heavy marble joggles a
foot square were sunk halfway into each course, the next course
being fitted over them to make a structure of immense strength
which Smeaton believed would last for ever.

The first stone was laid on 12 June 1757 and, although five
were lost, replacements were quickly recut from models at the
yard. Two gangs were employed, one working on the rock and one
at the yard. Work was completed two years later, after sixteen
working weeks on the rock, and to Smeaton's satisfaction the
tower was only one eighth of an inch from the perpendicular. In
all, 1,493 blocks of granite totalling 988 tons, 700 marble joggles,
1,800 thick oak trenails and 4,500 oak wedges were used in the

Eddystone: another view of the present lighthouse

construction and all 'without the loss of life or limb'.

Smeaton's lighthouse stood for 120 years, the light itself being gradually improved: first, twenty-four candles, then, in 1810, twenty-four oil lamps with reflectors behind them. In 1845 a dioptric lens with a single light source was installed.

As early as 1818, Robert Stevenson reported that the tower was in a dangerous state; waves had eroded the rock and undermined the lighthouse to such a degree he feared for the safety of the structure. However, it was not until the 1870s that Sir James Douglass, chief engineer to Trinity House, was instructed to design and build a new lighthouse.

The stump of Smeaton's tower still stands on the original rock; the upper portion can be seen on Plymouth Hoe, where it was re-erected as a memorial to its builder.

Sir James Douglass's light

From experience with Smeaton's lighthouse and Wolf Rock, James Douglass modified the basic design of his new tower. It had been found that when a tower rose in a curve from its foundation, powerful waves tended to swell up the structure, water often rising over the lantern and completely obscuring the light. To overcome this problem an immense solid foundation platform was built, 44ft in diameter and 22ft in height, with vertical sides. It was on this granite buffer that the waves would spend their energy before coming into contact with the curving walls of the tower. (Douglass used this design in the reconstruction of the Bishop Rock in 1887.)

Work began in July 1878 and by June of the following season the masons had completed underwater excavations and the construction of the cofferdam. The new tower was sited on a larger rock, some 40yds SSE from the old Eddystone. On 19 August the foundation stone was laid by HRH the Duke of Edinburgh, and by the end of that season eight courses were completed. In the subsequent year the tower rose to its thirty-eighth course, and on 1 June 1881 the Duke of Edinburgh laid the final stone of the tower. In all, 2,171 dovetailed stones, totalling 4,668 tons had been cut, transported to the reef and laid in place. A feature of the stones in the Douglass tower was that they were dovetailed not only to each other on all sides but each course was dovetailed to the next, calling for great accuracy from the masons.

Established 1703 (present tower 1882)
Height of light above MHW 135ft
Height of tower 168ft
Range 17.8 miles
W Gp Fl (10sec), 570,000cp
Optic 4th order catadioptric
Electricity, 100V 1,250W
Supertyfon fog horns (60sec) 3 blasts
No public access

START POINT

Start Point is one of the most exposed peninsulas on the English coast; it is a sharp headland running almost a mile into the sea on the south side of Start Bay. The lighthouse perches on the extremity and is approached by a narrow road cut out of the rock face, wide enough to take one car.

James Walker designed the lighthouse, considered at the time to be a fine example of construction. Two white lights were originally exhibited, one revolving and one fixed to mark the Skerries Rocks, but they were inadequate in fog and a bell was installed in the 1860s. The machinery was housed in a small building on the cliff face and operated by a weight which fell in a tube running down the sheer cliff. A siren replaced the bell after only fifteen years.

Start Point: the last patent for a lighthouse, issued in 1837, enabled Trinity House to build this station

An insight into the lighthouse and the life of its keepers in the nineteenth century is given in a travelogue by Walter White:

A substantial house, connected with the tall circular tower, in a walled enclosure, all nicely whitened, is the residence of the light-keepers. The buildings stand within a few yards of the verge of the cliff, the wall serving as a parapet, from which you look down on the craggy slope outside and the jutting rocks beyond — the outermost point. You may descend by the narrow path, protected also by a low white wall, and stride and scramble from rock to rock with but little risk of slipping, so rough are the surfaces with minute shells. A rude steep stair, chipped in the rock, leads down still lower to a little cove and a narrow strip of beach at the foot of the cliffs. It is the landing place for the lighthouse-keepers when they go fishing, but can only be used in calm weather.

The assistant-keeper spoke of the arrival of a visitor as a pleasure in the monotonous life of the establishment. Winter, he said, was a dreary time, not so much on account of cold, as of storms, fogs, and wild weather generally. In easterly gales the fury of the wind would often be such that to walk across the yard would be impossible; they had to crawl under shelter of the wall, and the spray flew from one side of the Point to the other. But indoors there was no lack of comfort, for the house was solidly built and conveniently fitted, and the Trinity Board kept a small collection of books circulating from lighthouse to lighthouse.

Established 1836
Height of light above MHW 204ft
Height of tower 92ft
Range 20.8 miles
W Gp Fl (10sec), 800,000cp
Optic small 3rd order catadioptric
Electricity, 100V 1,500W
Fog siren (60sec)
Open to public

Berry Head: the 'smallest, highest, and deepest' lighthouse in the British Isles

BERRY HEAD

Berry Head, designated as an area of outstanding natural beauty, is an extensive limestone headland. The near-perpendicular cliffs rise 200ft and the constant action of the waves has gouged out huge caverns. The plateau is green with plants, some of which are rare: pink thrift, white sea campion, autumn squill, wild rock rose, goldilocks and honewort. The rocks and cliffs abound with jackdaws, pigeons, kestrels, kittiwakes, gulls and guillemots. Fine views are to be had and it is possible on a clear day to see Portland Bill, over thirty-five miles away.

Torbay and Brixham Roads have long been sheltered anchorages, surrounded as they are by high hills and cliffs. Fortifications were erected on the headland in 1793 against threatened invasion by French armies and strengthened with limestone in 1803, when gun batteries were added to protect the anchorages. They were dismantled by 1820 and returned to civilian use, but the ramparts remain, overgrown with ivy.

At the end of Berry Head, beyond the coastguard station, is the lighthouse, which forms part of the chain of south coast beacons. It came to be known as the smallest, highest and deepest light in the British Isles — the tower is diminutive, requiring no further elevation than that given by the headland itself, and the optic was originally turned by the action of a weight falling down a 150ft-deep shaft, now made redundant by a small motor.

Established 1906
Height of light above MHW 191ft
Height of tower 15ft
Range 20 miles
W Gp Fl (15sec), 45,000cp
Optic 3rd order dioptric
Acetylene
No public access (unwatched)

PORTLAND BILL

Portland and Chesil Beach are the graveyards of many vessels that failed to reach Weymouth or Portland Roads. The Portland race is caused by the meeting of tides between the bill and the Shambles sandbank about 3 miles SE. Strong currents break the sea so fiercely that from the shore a continuous disturbance can be seen.

Portland Bill: the present tower replaces two earlier towers which dated from the beginning of the eighteenth century

As early as 1669 Sir John Clayton was granted a patent to erect a lighthouse, but his scheme fell through and it was not until early in the eighteenth century that Capt William Holman, supported by the shipowners and corporation of Weymouth, put a petition to Trinity House for the building of a lighthouse at Portland Bill. Trinity House opposed it, suggesting that lights at this point were needless and shipowners could not bear the burden of their upkeep. The people of Weymouth continued their petition and on 26 May 1716 Trinity House obtained a patent from George I. They in turn issued a lease for 61 years to a private consortium who built two lighthouses with enclosed lanterns and coal fires. The lights were badly kept, sometimes not lit at all, and in 1752 an inspection was made by two of the board of Trinity House who approached by sea to find 'it was nigh two hours after sunset before any light appeared in either of the lighthouses'. With the termination of the lease the lights reverted to Trinity House.

In 1789 William Johns, a builder of Weymouth under contract to Trinity House, took down one of the towers and erected a new one at a cost of £2,000. It was sited so that it served as a mark by day or night to direct ships moving up or down channel or into Portland Roads clear of the race and Shambles. Over the doorway on a marble tablet was the following inscription:

For the Direction and Comfort of NAVIGATORS; For the
Benefit and Security of COMMERCE and for a lasting
Memorial of BRITISH HOSPITALITY to All Nations
This lighthouse was erected by the Worshipful Brethren of
Trinity House of Deptford Strond   Anno 1789

In August 1788 Argand lamps were installed, Portland being the first lighthouse in England to be fitted with them. In the upper or old house there were two rows, seven in each row, lighted with oil and furnished with highly-polished reflectors. Low-light tests were made by Thomas Rogers with his new lens light, and six Argand lamps were installed, their lights increased by lenses.

In 1798, when Napoleon threatened to invade, two 18lb cannon were installed at the lighthouse.

Robert Stevenson visited the lighthouse in 1801.

New high and low lighthouses were built in 1869, but early this

Portland Bill: the original low light, now a private house

*Portland Bill: the original high light with lantern and gallery removed, now a
private house*

century Trinity House announced its intention of replacing them with a single tower — the present lighthouse. The old towers, which can still be seen, have been converted to private houses; the low light is much as it was in appearance but the high light lantern has been removed. Both are worth looking at from outside but there is of course no admittance.

Established 1906
Height of light above MHW 141ft
Height of tower 136ft
Range 18 miles
W Gp Fl (20sec), 3,370,000cp
Optic 1st order catadioptric
Electricity, 100V 3,000W
Diaphone fog signal (30sec)
Open to public

ANVIL POINT

Anvil Point is about midway between Portland Bill and the Needles; it is a picnickers' paradise. The ground floor of the lighthouse tower houses the controls for the fog signal, and stand-by generators fill the floor space.

The original optic, turned by clockwork, served from the establishment of the light until 1959 when the station was modernised.

Anvil Point: the site on Durlston Head is a picnickers' paradise

The station is reached by service road and lies about a mile south-west of Swanage; there is parking space on the headland.

The Tilly Whim caves, said to have been used by smugglers, are just below the lighthouse.

Established 1881
Height of light above MHW 149ft
Height of tower 39ft
Range 18.5 miles
W Fl (10sec), 500,000cp
Optic 4th order catadioptric
Electricity, 100V 1,000W
Tannoy fog horns (30sec) 3 blasts
Open to public

THE NEEDLES

Set in the western approaches to the Isle of Wight, the Needles form a narrow chalky peninsula which rises from jagged rocks to 400ft cliffs. These rocks have always been a hazard to shipping making its way up the Solent to Portsmouth and Southampton Water, and merchants and shipowners petitioned Trinity House for a lighthouse in 1781. Permission was granted in January 1782 when it was proposed that William Tatnall should at his own expense build the lighthouses, dwellings and necessary communicating roads, and provide keepers, at the Needles, St Catherine's Point and Hurst Point. All dues would go to Trinity House who in turn would pay Tatnall £960 a year for 21 years; alternatively, Trinity House would build the lights.

Negotiations must have failed because it was not until 1785 that Trinity House built the proposed lighthouses to the designs of R. Jupp. The light on the Needles was built on the summit of the cliff about 470ft above sea level. Ten Argand lamps and reflectors formed the light, which had a range of 11 miles and burned over 700 gallons of oil annually. As with other high towers, the light was often shrouded in sea mist so that it was of limited use to mariners, and Trinity House planned a new lighthouse to be built on the outermost of the chalk rocks near sea level. It was designed by James Walker and the cost was £20,000. Much of the

Needles: this tower was built to replace a clifftop light that was frequently obscured by fog

base rock was cut away to form the foundation, and cellars and storehouses were excavated in the chalk.

The red sector of the present light covers part of the approach to the St Anthony Rocks and the approach from the west to Needles Channel, dangerous to shipping because of the Dolphin Bank and the Shingles. The green sector marks a safe channel to sea past the Hatherwood Rocks.

Established 1859
Height of light above MHW 80ft
Height of tower 109ft
Range 14.7 miles
W R G Gp Occ (20sec), 35,000cp
Optic 2nd order catadioptric
Electricity, 100V 1,500W
Supertyfon fog horns (30sec) 2 blasts
No public access

HURST POINT

Following the failure of the negotiations with William Tatnall, Trinity House erected the lighthouse on the beach at Hurst Point in 1786. Shipping found the light good but it was obscured from certain directions, and to overcome this problem and also to provide leading lights a further lighthouse was built in 1812, also to the design of R. Jupp. In 1818 Robert Stevenson recorded that both towers were equipped with Argand lamps and parabolic reflectors and that each had reflectors to seaward as a leading light for the Shingles, and a further light towards Portsmouth. Both showed fixed white lights.

In 1866 a new lighthouse, the Low Light, was built to replace the old Hurst tower. The new station, a white circular granite tower, was discontinued on 30 November 1911 when a new light-

Hurst Point: though sited on the beach and easily accessible, this unmanned station is not open to the public

house with a square tower was completed on Hurst Castle. This tower is known today as Hurst Front and the light established in 1812 is Hurst Rear.

Established 1812
Height of light above MHW 49ft
(Hurst Front) 76ft (Hurst Rear)
Height of tower 52ft (Hurst
Front) 85ft (Hurst Rear)
Range 12.5 miles (Hurst Front)
14.4 miles (Hurst Rear)
W R Iso (4sec Hurst Front, 6sec
Hurst Rear), 11,000/10,000cp
Optic 1st order catadioptric
(both towers)
Acetylene (both towers)
No public access (unwatched)

ST CATHERINE'S POINT

East of the Needles the coast of the Isle of Wight forms a large bay indented by smaller ones and sweeps round to St Catherine's Point. Each of these sandy bays forms a distinctive feature of the coastline, being enclosed first of all by cliffs of chalk and further on by sandstone. The sandstone cliffs are one of the attractions of the island, as sands of many colours can be found beneath them. The cliffs rise steeply towards St Catherine's Down where the headland is over 300ft in height.

The loss of a vessel carrying a cargo of wine from a monastery in Picardy in 1314 led to the building of the first lighthouse on the point. Walter de Godeton, a wealthy merchant, bought most of the ultimately stolen cargo, but in 1323 the news of his dealings came to the ears of the pope with the result that in atonement for buying the wine de Godeton established in the hermitage on St Catherine's Point a priest to offer continual prayer for those who perished at sea. He also built a tower from which a coal-fired light was displayed each night. Both services continued until 1536 when, with the suppression of the monasteries by Henry VIII, the hermitage and light were destroyed.

St Catherine's Point: 'the cow and calf'

In 1785 a new lighthouse was started by Trinity House, but the project was abandoned before completion owing to the mists which so frequently envelop the hill.

The present lighthouse was designed by Messrs Walker & Burgess of London. Built of ashlar stone with dressed quoins, it was a 120ft three-tier octagon. When completed, the lighthouse with its castellated gallery parapet must have been a fine example of coastal architecture, but the elevation of the light again proved to be too great and the lantern was frequently shrouded in mist. In 1875, therefore, the decision was made to lower the light 43ft by removing 20ft from the uppermost section of the tower and 23ft from the middle tier. This completely destroyed its beauty. The light was fuelled initially by sperm oil and then by rape oil, and in 1875 a new lamp was installed, a 6in burner using paraffin oil which doubled the intensity of the light. Between 1887-8 a power-ful electric light based on cored carbon arc lamps, was installed, the electricity being generated at the lighthouse.

Up to 1932 the fog signal was sited near the edge of the cliff, but erosion and cliff movement began to cause serious cracks in the building. A new fog signal house was joined to the lighthouse tower, designed to match the existing architectural pattern and looking like a smaller replica, with its castellated parapet reproduced in miniature. This greatly improved the appearance of the lighthouse but earned it the local nickname of 'the cow and calf'.

Established 1840
Height of light above MHW 136ft
Height of tower 84ft
Range 17.8 miles
W Fl (5sec), 5,250,000cp
Optic 2nd order catadioptric
Electricity, 100V 3,000W
Supertyfon fog horns (45sec)
Open to public

NAB TOWER

The Nab Tower is a large concrete fortress at the western entrance to the Solent, well known to local yachtsmen. It was built during World War 1 with the intention of forming an anti-submarine barrage of cables and nets stretched across the Solent. The lights, one on each side of the tower, were added after the war.

Before the fortress was built, the Nab Rock, on which it stands, was marked by a lightship moored in 1812.

Established 1920
Height of light above MHW 80ft
Height of tower 92ft
Range 14.7 miles
1W 1R Fl (10sec), R 10,000/W 100,000cp
Optic 5th order dioptric
Electricity, 100V 1,000W (outer),
    100V 500W (inner)
Diaphone fog signal (60sec) and bell (7.5sec)
No public access

BEACHY HEAD

It is said that as early as 1670 a light shone from the top of the cliffs at Beachy Head, the 300ft seaward termination of the Sussex Downs. On this point James Walker erected a circular stone tower in 1828, 47ft high and frequently obscured by sea mist even when the atmosphere below was comparatively clear. The lighthouse remained in operation until 1899 when it was felt that it was endangered by the disintegration of the cliff face and that a new and lower light was needed in any case.

Materials being transported by cableway during the building of Beachy Head lighthouse

A survey of the seabed revealed an excellent foundation in hard chalk about 550ft from the base of the cliffs. As the site was submerged at high tide a cofferdam was erected which enabled the builders to work safely for long stretches at a time. When the water level fell below the upper rim, the water inside was immediately pumped out and work began again. A hole 10ft deep was excavated in the solid rock to receive the footings of the tower; blasting was not possible as it would have shattered the hard crust of the seabed.

A strong iron staging was built adjoining the dam and from this point to the top of the cliffs was stretched a cableway which carried materials and workmen to the site. The span was about 600ft, and the cables (one of which was 6in in diameter and had a breaking strain of 120 tons) safely carried the dressed stones for the lower courses, some weighing as much as five tons.

Beachy Head: profile of the beautifully proportioned tower

The base of the lighthouse is solid for its first fifty or so feet except for a storage space for drinking water. In the construction of the tower, 3,660 tons of Cornish granite were used; it took two years to complete.

> Established 1828 (present tower 1902)
> Height of light above MHW 103ft
> Height of tower 142ft
> Range 25 miles
> W Gp Fl (20sec), 880,000cp
> Optic 1st order catadioptric
> Electricity, 240V 400W
> Electric fog signal (30sec)
> No public access

ROYAL SOVEREIGN

Where the English Channel narrows into the Strait of Dover, hazards to shipping are encountered. Shoals and sandbanks lie in the path of coastal vessels, stretching from the Royal Sovereign and the Varne shoals through the Goodwin Sands and thence along the eastern seaboard of England to beyond Spurn Head. Some extend twenty miles out to sea and are completely submerged at high water. It was for centuries considered impossible to supply reliable and permanent warning of these hidden perils, but in the eighteenth and nineteenth centuries wooden vessels which exhibited lights were moored to mark the sands. They often dragged their chains, to be wrecked on the sands, but they marked the beginning of an efficient lightship service.

Trinity House maintained a light-vessel to mark the Royal Sovereign Shoal from 1875, but in line with their policy of replacing lightships with more economical seamarks Trinity House in 1966 commissioned Sir William Halcrow & Partners to investigate and report upon the feasibility of a light tower structure for this site and subsequently appointed them as consulting engineers for the project. Tenders were invited in 1966 for a steel structure; the lowest, that of Christiani & Nielsen, proposed an alternative scheme in concrete, which was accepted.

The whole structure except for the steel lantern tower is built in reinforced concrete of a high-density type with a life of at least fifty years. It is designed to withstand the most severe storms which can be predicted, with waves breaking fifty feet high and winds in excess of 110 knots.

The base and tower were constructed in a basin excavated behind the storm crest of the beach at Newhaven, work being started in 1967, but in November of that year the sea broke through, carrying shingle into the works and halting progress for three months while restoration and cleaning took place. Work on the tower was completed late in 1968. It was made in two parts, one telescoped inside the other, so that it would be stable when towed to sea. In the summer of 1969, the shingle between the sea and the basin was breached and the base unit towed out and grounded a few hundred yards off in the bay to await completion of the sea-bed foundation. It was finally towed to the shoal on 11 and 12 June 1970, accurately positioned, and sunk on to the prepared bed, work beginning at once to consolidate the foundation.

The cabin section was built on the beach at Newhaven and, after the base unit had been moved, was rolled on to a temporary pier in the basin to allow two pontoons to float underneath. In the spring of 1971 the cabin, supported on the pontoons, was taken from the basin and towed to an Admiralty mooring in Portsmouth Harbour, the nearest suitable sheltered water, from whence it could be taken at short notice to the site. The first attempt was made on 12 May but the weather deteriorated and the tugs had to turn back. A second attempt was made on 15 May, and early next morning the cabin arrived at the site to be moored near the base and tower. At high tide it was pulled over the tower and the two parts married accurately; the pontoons were then towed away. The last and most difficult operation was to jack up the inner, telescoped tower and lift the cabin 45ft to its proper height. Later, the outer part of the tower was extended upwards 12ft with concrete brought by helicopter from Eastbourne.

Accommodation is provided for three keepers and four visiting mechanics, with all-electric kitchen, sitting room with television, a hobby room, laundry and a deep freeze unit. The roof of the cabin serves as a flight deck for the relief helicopter. The total cost of the lighthouse was £1,600,000.

Five thousand gallons of diesel oil for the generators and 9,000 gallons of fresh water are stored on the station, which is provided with VHF and MF radio-telephone communication equipment. A marine radio beacon is installed.

Royal Sovereign: a new dimension in lighthouse engineering — a tower where only lightships could be stationed

Established 1971
Height of light above MHW 93ft
Height of tower 159ft
Range 28 miles
W F (20sec), 2,500,000cp
Optic 3rd order catadioptric
Electricity, 100V 1,000W
Diaphone fog signal (30sec) 2 blasts
No public access

DUNGENESS

Dungeness lies at the southernmost point of Kent and is an enormous flat of sand and shingle, treacherous to sailors. In one winter gale over 1,000 seamen lost their lives on the ness, and merchandise to the value of £100,000 was lost with them. The steeple of Lydd church, distinct against the sky, appeared like 'the forme of the saile of some talle shippe' and lured many vessels on to the sand in the reign of James I.

Dungeness was thus an obvious site for a lighthouse, and Sir Edward Howard, one of the king's cupbearers, obtained a patent with permission to levy a toll of one penny a ton on all ships passing the light for the next forty years. Trinity House opposed the grant but James I gave the licence in August 1615. Howard found it well nigh impossible to collect the dues for the upkeep of his open coal fire, although the advantages to navigation were immediately obvious, and he sold his lease to William Lamplough, clerk of the king's kitchen, who wisely enlisted the help of customs officers to collect tolls at the ports where they were represented. With the support of the shipowners, who could no longer get away with non-payment of dues, Trinity House tried to get the patent cancelled as a 'nuisance to navigation'. This was in 1621, and Lamplough was warned to keep a better light. By this time candles were being used instead of coal, but gave a very poor light. In 1635, after complaints that the light was at too great a distance from the sea, Lamplough built a new tower to seaward and reverted to a coal fire.

For a hundred years the fire was kindled on the tower at Dungeness, but during Oliver Cromwell's ascendancy the patent was taken from Lamplough and the landowner threatened the new patentee that he would demolish the lighthouse if arrears in rent were not forthcoming. The owner appealed for and received government protection but was warned about the quality of his light in 1668. By 1746, the shape of the flat had altered, leaving

Dungeness: the new lighthouse (left) was opened in 1961 by HRH the Duke of Gloucester: the 1904 tower (right) with base of 1792 tower in front

the lighthouse far from the water's edge, which led to many complaints. It became obvious that a new lighthouse was needed.

Samuel Wyatt designed and built a new tower in 1792, about 116ft in height and similar in design to Smeaton's Eddystone, and equipped with eighteen sperm oil lamps which replaced the old coal fire. It suffered severe damage in a storm one Christmas day in the nineteenth century and the whole structure was then hooped like a barrel. An electric light was installed in 1862, making the station one of the first in England to be electrified. The outer wall of the tower was painted black with a broad white band.

By 1895 the lighthouse, originally sited about 100yd from the water's edge, stood over 500yd from the shore and it was felt that another lighthouse was needed on the ness. Work began in 1901 and the tower was completed and lit on 31 March 1904.

The nuclear power station built in the 1950s obscured the lighthouse and necessitated the construction of yet another, the present tower, a superb example of engineering. It is built with interlocking precast concrete rings, twenty-one in all, each penetrated vertically by stressing wires which run from the top of the tower to the base, where they are held under tension. The wires give the thin-walled structure the strength to withstand great stresses and eliminated the need for a massive building. Tannoy emitters are a feature of the upper section of the tower.

The optic was the first to incorporate a xenon electric arc lamp, later replaced with a sealed beam unit when it proved unsatisfactory. A radio beacon transmits direction-finding information to shipping, and the whole tower is floodlit externally to improve identification from seaward. The floodlighting has reduced the numbers of birds killed by flying into the lantern during migration.

Trinity House use Dungeness as their experimental station.

Established 1792 (present tower 1961)
Height of light above MHW 135ft
Height of tower 140ft
Range 27 miles
W Fl (10sec), floodlit
Electricity, 56V 180W
Tannoy fog horns (30sec) 3 blasts
Open to public (base only)

DOVER

The remains of a Roman pharos thought to date from the first century AD are to be seen at Dover; it is the survivor of two towers, one on the Western Heights and the other beside the castle where the square base and 80ft tower still stand. The stone superstructure formed a platform for the wood or coal-fired light about 400ft above the sea.

The Dover Harbour Board maintain the modern light on the Admiralty Pier extension; it is 71ft high with a range of 20 miles and has a diaphone fog signal. On the Prince of Wales pier head another tower, 45ft high, shows a fixed green light with a range of 4 miles. The pier head has an attractive restaurant which gives a panoramic view of the channel.

SOUTH FORELAND

The white chalk cliffs of South Foreland rise 300ft and overlook a most dangerous stretch of water. The danger to shipping is not from rocks or currents but from vast stretches of sand in almost continuous shoals and banks. The most notorious are the Goodwin Sands, which extend ten miles north to south and three miles east to west. In the deep water between the Goodwins and the mainland, the Downs, vessels lie at anchor protected from easterly and westerly gales. The Goodwins claimed innumerable tons of shipping and the lives of many crewmen. A storm of 1836 caused the loss of thirty vessels.

Shipowners, dismayed by loss of life and cargo, in 1634 petitioned for a lighthouse on the South Foreland to indicate the position of the sands (lightships were not in common use until about 1795). Trinity House opposed the petition, saying that in their opinion no lights were required and arguing that the introduction of a toll would be a 'grievance to navigation'. They claimed that they would have built a lighthouse had they thought it necessary.

Charles I nevertheless granted permission in 1634 to Sir John Meldrum to erect two lighthouses with beacon fires to warn vessels off the Goodwin Sands, and under the patent Sir John also received permission to build a further light at the North Foreland. The patent was to run for fifty years at an annual rent of £20. At the

South Foreland: one of the first British lighthouses to be powered by electricity

South Foreland he built a high and a low light of timber and plaster, the former sited well back from the cliff edge and the latter some 75ft from it. The open fires were enclosed in 1719 but the light was poor and shipowners complained so bitterly that in 1730 the lanterns were removed and the lights left as open coal fires. Keeping the fires going on windy evenings must have been hard work, and the keepers must have been relieved when in 1793 the lanterns were again enclosed and sperm-oil lamps with reflectors were installed. Robert Stevenson, on his visit to the lighthouse in 1818, described the apparatus as holding twelve to fourteen plated reflectors which were not thoroughly clean but noted: 'The dwelling houses partake of that cleanliness which is so general in the cottages of the English.' The annual profit from the dues amounted to £1,000.

The upper lighthouse was completely rebuilt in 1843 to the design of James Walker, chief engineer to Trinity House. The lower lighthouse was rebuilt in 1846. They formed a leading light visible from the southern end of the Goodwins. The lower tower was put out of use early this century and is now only feet away from the eroded cliff edge.

Many lighting experiments were carried out at South Foreland between 1858 and 1885. The strongest artificial light known,

Professor Holmes's magneto-electric lamp, was tested but it was not until fifteen years had passed that the electrical system finally replaced oil. Holmes's lamp was followed by Dr Siemens's dynamo, which was considerably more efficient. Experiments with coal gas as a source of light were carried out over a number of years, and tests were made of the efficiency of sirens and gunshots as fog signals.

The use of radio communication as an aid to navigation was first attempted here by Marconi in 1898, on Christmas eve, and contact made with the East Goodwin lightship ten miles away. It was used the following spring to summon help to the stricken lightship when the steamship *R. F. Matthews* ran her down.

> Established 1793 (present tower 1843)
> Height of light above MHW 374ft
> Height of tower 69ft
> Range 26.6 miles
> W Gp Fl (20sec), 1,000,000cp
> Optic 2nd order dioptric
> Electricity, 100V 3,500W
> No public access (unwatched)

NORTH FORELAND

Sir John Meldrum's patent of 1634 empowered him to collect dues of one penny a ton from British and twopence a ton from foreign vessels passing the North and South Forelands. The North Foreland tower, similar in construction to its partner across the bay, was burned to the ground in 1683 and replaced temporarily by a single candle placed in a glass lantern on a pole. A coal-fired beacon was built ten years later and this too was burned soon after it was first lit. As much as 100 tons of coal were consumed annually while the light operated, and the keepers were expected to keep the light bright on calm evenings by constant use of bellows. They were paid £13 a year, with a free cottage and coal.

Later, an octagonal tower was built of brick and stone, and part of it can be seen in the present structure. It was coal-fired, and open until the trustees enclosed the lights of both North and South Forelands in lanterns in 1719. Shipowners complained of the con-

North Foreland: it is claimed that England's earliest lighthouse was situated here

dition of the light, but the glass could not be kept clean and the lanterns were taken away in 1730, the open fires remaining for another sixty years.

Trinity House took over the responsibility for the Forelands lights in 1832 and restored and improved them soon afterwards. The North Foreland tower was designated in 1950 as a building of historic interest.

Established 1790
Height of light above MHW 188ft
Height of tower 85ft
Range 20.1 miles
W R Gp Fl (20sec), 175,000cp
Optic 1st order catadioptric
Electricity, 240V 3,000W
Open to public

THE CHANNEL ISLANDS

(Map B p 28)

The Channel Islands are separated from mainland Britain by the English Channel; the four major islands are Guernsey, Jersey, Alderney and Sark. A dozen miles or so of shallow, rock-strewn water lie between Jersey and the coast of Normandy, and Alderney is only six miles from Cap de la Hague. Sharp reefs present the greatest hazard to shipping in this area, the most dangerous being the Casquets off the coast of Alderney; other equally dangerous groups lie off the coasts of Jersey and Guernsey, respectively the Corbière and Hanois Rocks. These islands were known in the eighteenth and nineteenth centuries as the 'graveyard of the Channel'. Jersey and Guernsey each has its own parliament, which was responsible for the erection and maintenance of two major lighthouses: la Corbière and Platte Fougére. Trinity House erected the tower on the Hanois Rocks and the stations on Sark and Alderney. The lighting of the Casquets was accomplished much earlier.

CASQUETS

The Casquets lie about midway in the shipping lanes between England and Brittany and are extremely difficult to approach. Only on calm days when the wind is favourable can a landing be made, and relief of the lighthouse keepers is often delayed by harsh conditions. In his diary of 1818, Robert Stevenson described the site as 'a barren sandstone rock about 100 fathoms in length, rough and irregular in the extreme and rising about 100ft in height'. The rocks are frequently shrouded in fog.

Shipowners and merchants who had suffered the loss of valuable vessels and cargoes approached Thomas le Cocq, then owner of the rocks, to build a lighthouse and offered to pay him a halfpenny per ton of cargo when their ships passed the light. In turn, le Cocq petitioned Trinity House and was granted a patent in 1723. The lease was for 61 years at an annual rent of £50. Three towers were built, each showing a coal fire set in a glazed lantern, and it was hoped to distinguish this station from any other on the English and French coastline; the towers became known as St Peter, St Thomas and Dungeon. The first fires were kindled on 30 October 1724.

The Casquets: all three towers originally showed lights

The lease expired and passed in 1785 to Trinity House who five years later installed Argand lamps with polished metal reflectors. These were superseded in 1818 when all three towers were equipped with revolving apparatus. Stevenson comments: 'They appeared too close and indeed exhibited only two lights. The lightrooms are intended to be all of the same height from the sea — perhaps 130ft or 150ft — but were too low so the lights were hid by the largeness of the diameter of the towers.' Seamen rarely saw all three lights, as they were not synchronised. In 1854 the towers were rebuilt and increased in height by 30ft, but two of the lights were discontinued in 1877 although the towers still stand.

The steam ship *Stella* went aground on the Casquets in 1899 with the loss of 112 lives; one child was saved because his mother had tied his new football around his collar. In 1744, the British man o'war *Victory* ran on to the rocks with the loss of 1,100 lives.

Established 1723
Height of light above MHW 120ft
Height of tower 75ft
Range 17 miles

W Gp Fl (30sec), 2,830,000cp
Optic 2nd order catadioptric
Electricity, 100V 3,000W
Diaphone fog signals (60sec) 2 blasts
No public access

ALDERNEY: QUÉNARD POINT

The rock station at Quénard Point in the north-east of the island
was established nearly two centuries after the Casquets lights.
Though isolated and classed as a rock station, it is in fact accessible
to the public. Relief is by helicopter.

*Quénard Point: a popular attraction for tourists and a staging post for
migrating birds*

The well-proportioned tower, white with a central black band, is
a gathering ground for migrating birds.

Established 1912
Height of light above MHW 121ft
Height of tower 106ft
Range 17 miles

W Gp Fl (15sec), 458,000cp
Optic 1st order catadioptric
Paraffin vapour
Fog siren (60sec) 4 blasts
Open to public

SARK: POINT ROBERT

Sark is the smallest of the Channel Islands, about two miles wide
by three miles long, and the lighthouse stands in the south-east part.
It appears to be a land station but, like Quénard Point, is classed as
a rock station because of its inaccessibility; keepers on duty here
must spend the time away from their families.

Point Robert: this is one of the few rock stations open to the public

The lighthouse and outbuildings cling to the face of the cliff
which rises steeply above.

Modernisation was carried out in 1969 and the electricity which
powers the apparatus is generated on site, all systems being dupli-
cated in case of failure.

84

Established 1913
Height of light above MHW 213ft
Height of tower 55ft
Range 28.5 miles
W Fl (15sec), 2,800,000cp
Optic 2nd order catadioptric
Electricity, 100V 1,500W
Nautophone fog horn (30sec) 2 blasts
Open to public

GUERNSEY: PLATTE FOUGÉRE

This lighthouse was the result of many years' development work in lighthouse technology by the famous Scottish family of engineers, the Stevensons. It marks the entrance to the Russell Channel which leads into St Peter Port, the capital of Guernsey. At the head of the channel, rocks like Grande Braye, Brasier and Platte Fougére, with strong tidal currents running among them, are a danger to shipping. Merchants and shipowners frequently petitioned the States Parliament for a sound signal by night and in foggy weather. General Campbell, Governor-General of Guernsey, approached David and Charles Stevenson who surveyed the site and made their recommendations. The island could not afford a rock lighthouse such as the Eddystone or Bishop Rock, estimated to cost £60,000, and the engineers suggested instead an automatic light and fog signal on the Platte Fougére, controlled by submarine cable from the mainland.

Much of the foundation work was carried out under water. The base was made from Portland cement cast in iron moulds and strengthened with iron bars and two rooms were built above the solid section, the first at entrance level for the electric motors and an air compressor, the second for duplicate equipment. The fog siren projects through the top of the tower and is fed from three compressed-air storage tanks which, like the lantern and acetylene plant for the light, are situated on the top. The tower is grey with a black band.

Maintained by French lighthouse authorities
Height of tower 83ft
Range 16 miles

W Fl (10sec)
Acetylene/electricity (controlled from
    Fort Doyle by submarine cable)
Fog siren (93sec)
No public access (unwatched)

GUERNSEY: LES HANOIS

The lighthouse rises from a reef on the south-west side of Guernsey
and takes its name from a group of rocks, Les Hanois. It is important in the development of lighthouse engineering because, like the
Douglass Eddystone of 1882, all the stones in each course, and the
courses themselves, were dovetailed together to form one solid mass.
Various methods of jointing the stones in rock towers have been
tried: Smeaton developed the use of granite blocks connected with
metal and wooden pins and marble joggles or dowels. Alan
Stevenson used a similar method in the construction of the
Skerryvore lighthouse, and his father, Robert, arranged the stones
in each course of the Bell Rock so that they formed a series of
dovetails. In this manner each course locked together into a single
unit, and the courses were then pinned together. Nicholas Douglass
suggested that stones might be dovetailed together both laterally
and vertically. The cement mortar in the joints locked the dovetails
so hard that they cannot be separated without breaking the stones.
This method was first employed at the Hanois lighthouse and
became the pattern for all sea rock towers.

The present electric lamp was installed in 1962, with a first
stand-by of batteries and a second of a paraffin vapour burner.

Established 1862
Height of light above MHW 102ft
Height of tower 117ft
Range 16 miles
W Gp Fl (5sec), 400,000cp
Optic 4th order catadioptric
Electricity, 100V 1,000W
Supertyfon fog horns (60sec) 2 blasts
No public access

86

JERSEY: LA CORBIÈRE

La Corbière is a reef extending half a mile into the sea from the south-west tip of Jersey. It is a popular tourist spot but also a dangerous place, and a granite plaque on the wall near the causeway that leads across to the lighthouse reminds visitors of one of the keepers, Peter Larbalestier, who was drowned while attempting to save a holidaymaker.

The reef, rounded by all vessels coming from the mainland and the other islands and bound for St Helier, has always been a danger to shipping. In 1309 it was recorded that a tub was washed ashore from a wreck at Corbière, and in 1414 a 'great Spanish ship was lost on the Corbière and the sands of St Ouen's Bay were strewn with casks of wine'. In 1495, five Spanish caravels came to grief there and in 1859 the mail steamer *Express* hit the reef and sank.

The States Parliament called upon architect Sir John Coode and engineer Imrie Bell in 1873 to plan a lighthouse to safeguard the reef. The construction was unusual for its time; thus was the first tower in Britain to be built entirely of concrete.

The station is connected to the mainland by a causeway which is covered at high tide.

La Corbière: one of the first concrete lighthouses

Maintained by French lighthouse authorities
Established 1873
Height of light above MHW 119ft
Height of tower 62ft
Range 18 miles
W R Iso (10sec), 51,000cp, dioptric
Electricity, 100V 1,000W
Diaphone fog signal (60sec)
Open to public

THE EAST COAST

Orfordness to Whitby (Map C p 29)

Roker Pier to Longstone (Map D p 30)

ORFORDNESS

When ships pass the South Foreland on a northerly route across the Thames estuary, they enter waters in which dangers are not immediately obvious. The coast lacks distinctive landmarks, and constant tidal movement has thrown up sandbanks like the 13-mile spit which roughly parallels the marshy coastline of Orford. Wrecks along this stretch were numerous, particularly at Orfordness where, during a single night of storm in 1627, thirty-two ships are recorded as having been lost.

Orfordness: this unmanned light is best seen from the village of Orford, half a mile away

The existing lights — two huts with installations of candles — were nevertheless of such benefit to shipping that Charles I granted a patent to Gerald Gore, a London alderman, to build permanent lighthouses on the ness. The patent ran until 1720 when it passed to an owner who pulled down the timber towers, which were decaying, and replaced them by brick towers. The lower tower was washed away after only four years, as was the timber construction which followed. The tower was again rebuilt but burned down in 1731; its replacement suffered the same fate the following year.

Presumably suffering from discouragement and heavy expense, the owner did not replace the tower immediately. A new light was operating by the early 1740s, however, and both towers now had lanterns enclosing a coal fire in one and an oil lamp in the other. Argand burners and reflectors were fitted in 1793.

Trinity House was authorised in 1836 to purchase patents of coastal lighthouses still in private hands, and Orfordness, with thirteen years to run, cost them £37,896, a sum which gives some idea of the potential profitability of an important light at that time.

Fifty years after the acquisition, the lower tower was taken out of use and a new light established instead at Southwold. The keepers were withdrawn when the lighthouse was electrified and made fully automatic in 1959, and it is now controlled by landline from the Trinity House depot at Harwich.

The nearest point of access is Orford, where the lighthouse can be seen about half a mile away across the ness, but it is not possible to approach it as it lies within the restricted area of a government establishment.

> Established 1792
> Height of light above MHW 93ft
> Height of tower 99ft
> Range 15.5 miles
> W Fl (5sec), 7,500,000cp
> Optic 2nd order catadioptric
> Electricity, 100V 3,000W
> No public access (unwatched)

SOUTHWOLD

Southwold is a charming Suffolk seaside resort midway between Lowestoft to the north and Orford to the south. The pleasant, painted houses and the many open greens give the town its character and a feeling of spaciousness. It is situated on a gentle slope rising from the Blyth valley, and the towers of the church and the lighthouse dominate the landscape for miles around.

Trinity House established the fine lighthouse and the wall facing the entrance bears their coat of arms. It was built in the mid-

Southwold: the tower stands close to the town centre

Victorian period of lighthouse construction when an attempt was
made to light the whole coast of Britain. The round white tower
stands close to the centre of the town. It is not an extensive station,
with keepers' dwellings as at Lowestoft and elsewhere; the only
building adjoining the tower is a small entrance and service room,
and the impression is that the lighthouse was built in a back garden.
The tower is imposing, and its grandeur of scale is emphasised by
the small houses that crowd around it. The light was originally
from Argand burners until electricity was laid on in 1938. The red
sectors mark shoals to the north, and the Sizewell Bank, and the
main navigation light is white.

> Established 1890
> Height of light above MHW 120ft
> Height of tower 101ft
> Range 17 miles
> W R Gp Fl (20sec), 243,000cp
> Optic 1st order catadioptric
> Electricity, 240V 3,000W
> No public access (unwatched)

92

LOWESTOFT

In 1609, Trinity House responded to petitions from shipowners and merchants who had lost men, cargoes and vessels, and whose proposal was to erect two towers, a high and low light, 'for the direction of ships which crept by night in the dangerous passage betwixt Lowestoft and Winterton'. A substantial tower was therefore built in April 1609 on the clifftop overlooking Lowestoft, and another on the ness 100ft below. Both were equipped with glazed lanterns and the lights were tallow candles. Repairs were required twelve years later, and in 1628 the high light was completely rebuilt.

The present lighthouse dates from 1676, when Trinity House erected a new high light at a cost of £300 and removed the original lantern in order to instal an open grate for a coal-fired light. This caused uproar in the town as dangerous sparks were being carried to buildings only eighty yards away, and Trinity House was compelled to erect a glazed lantern which greatly reduced the effectiveness of the light. As much as forty tons of coal were consumed annually here, and as at all such towers work must have been hard and uncomfortable for the keepers.

This tower became known as the Pepys tower, from the inscription that it was erected during the mastership of Samuel Pepys. The arms of Trinity House, customarily mounted on all its lighthouses, can be seen.

Trinity House recorded in 1777 that experiments were made with reflector lights at Lowestoft. The coal fire in the high light was replaced by a new glass lantern 7ft high and 6ft in diameter, inside which was a large cylinder covered with 4,000 small mirrors to reflect the light from 126 oil lamps arranged in a circle. This must have led to a considerable saving in maintenance. The spangle light, as it was known, was said to have a range of twenty miles. The development of lighthouse optics at this period was rapid and by 1796 the spangle light had been abandoned and Argand lamps and silvered parabolic reflectors installed.

The high light was further modernised in 1874 and in 1899 a new optic was installed and the lantern enlarged to its present size.

The low light was rebuilt many times. It was abandoned in 1706 when it was being undermined by the sea but shipowners pressed for a replacement which was eventually built about twenty years

Lowestoft: the station borders a main road through the town

later. A fog bell was installed in 1866 and replaced by a fog horn, with the bell as stand-by, in 1894. The station was finally discontinued in 1923 and its function today is carried on by a fog signal on the South Pier head.

The high light is one of the longest-established stations in use.

> Established 1609 (present tower 1676)
> Height of light above MHW 123ft
> Height of tower 53ft
> Range 17.2 miles
> W Fl (15sec), 2,000,000cp
> Optic 4th order twin catadioptric
> Electricity, 100V 1,000W
> Open to public

GORLESTON

Although Gorleston was mentioned in a 1676 treatise on sea law, in a reference to the 'great and pious care' of Charles II in granting permission for a lighthouse there 'at his own princely charge', the

94

tower was in fact built elsewhere. Harbour lighthouses were erected at Yarmouth Haven from 1852 onwards, but they were purely local and tide lights. The structure at Brush Bend, Gorleston, built in 1878, is a circular red-brick tower 70ft in height. The light is fixed red with a range of 6 miles. There is a secondary white leading light, with a range of 10 miles, 24ft high in the same tower.

Two keepers maintained the original light; now unmanned, it functions as a pilots' lookout post. It is a quaint tower, well worth seeing among its incongruous modern neighbours: souvenir and fish-and-chip shops.

HAPPISBURGH

Happisburgh — or 'Haisbro' as it is known locally — has a fine lighthouse standing in the centre of a field about half a mile from the shore. It is the high light of the original pair of towers.

Henry Taylor was responsible for the first proposals to build a lighthouse at Happisburgh. Trinity House built two towers in 1791, the present one and another on the cliff edge some 400yd north of Cart Gap. They were designed by Mr Green of Norwich. The early

Happisburgh: for a short period in the 1860s, coal gas made on the site powered this light experimentally

lights, which may have been candle-powered, were replaced by Argand lamps and reflectors, manufactured in London by George Robinson and Robert Wilkins. The two lighthouses replaced the old Caistor lights, which were closed down.

The high light was altered from a fixed beacon to an occulting light and, having stationed an extra lightvessel to guard the Haisbro Sands, Trinity House closed down the clifftop low light, which was demolished in 1883. Sir James Douglass renovated the high light in 1884, and it remained in service virtually unchanged until 1929 when it was made automatic.

The remains of the old clifftop tower can be seen a few hundred yards away: a circular wall of brick, a pile of slate slabs from the staircase, and the stone floors of the dwellings.

Happisburgh was the site of early experiments with coal gas lighting and this form of power was introduced temporarily in 1865, the gas being made on the premises.

> Established 1791
> Height of light above MHW 136ft
> Height of tower 85ft
> Range 17.8 miles
> W Gp Fl (30sec), 58,500cp
> Optic 1st order catadioptric
> Electricity, 240V 500W
> No public access (unwatched)

CROMER

Before the erection of a lighthouse at Cromer, or Foulness as it once was called, lights for the guidance of vessels were shown from the tower of the parish church. They were only small but served a useful purpose for many years. After the failure of a projected lighthouse in 1690 (the tower was built but a light never kindled), Nathaniel Life, owner of the land at Foulness, thought it essential to have a lighthouse there and in 1717 built a new tower (or perhaps kindled a light on the existing tower) and was granted a patent in 1719, the dues to be one farthing per ton on general cargo and one halfpenny per chaldron (25½cwt) of Newcastle coal. The patent specified that after sixty-one years the land and lighthouse should pass to Trinity House. The annual rent was £100.

Cromer: the small lantern, installed in the late 1950s, replaced a structure of pleasanter proportions

The light was coal-fired, enclosed in a glass lantern, and was kindled on 29 September 1719. In 1792, on the expiry of the lease, Trinity House fitted a flashing light of five reflectors and Argand oil lamps on each of three surfaces of a revolving frame.

The sea encroached rapidly and the two young women keepers must have feared often for the safety of the structure. In 1799, 1825 and 1852 immense masses of the cliff slipped into the sea and at last the lighthouse was declared unsafe. In 1866 a landslip finally destroyed the deserted tower.

The present lighthouse, a white eight-sided tower, stands on the golf course about half a mile from the cliff edge.

> Established 1719 (present tower 1833)
> Height of light above MHW 274ft
> Height of tower 58ft
> Range 23.4 miles
> W Gp Fl (15sec), 98,000cp
> Optic 3rd order catadioptric
> Electricity, 240V 1,500W
> Open to public

HUNSTANTON POINT

In 1663 the mayor of Lynn, supported by 183 shipowners petitioned Charles II for the issue of a patent for the erection of lighthouses at Hunstanton. The Wash is bordered by sandbanks that stretch over four miles to sea, and it was through these that the Old Lynn Channel formed a passage for vessels; the petition noted that 'Many have perished upon the same sands especially in the night, which might, by God's blessing easily be prevented by the erection of lights upon a place called Hunstanton Cliff or Chapel lands in the said County of Norfolk.' The shipowners were prepared to pay dues of eightpence on every twenty tons of coal or other goods and one penny per ton on the cargo of foreign vessels. The petition was passed to Trinity House who issued a certificate of approval; a patent was formally granted in 1665.

Hunstanton Point: the lighthouse as it was in 1922, the year in which it was closed; it is now a private house

Two stone lighthouses were built at a cost of £210 and set in line to show the channel through the sandbanks. The grant was extended in 1709, to the annoyance of Trinity House who expected it to pass to them, and the legal proceedings cost the owner three years' profits. The inner light was coal-burning, the outer was fitted with candles, and annual profits after maintenance amounted to £43.

The rear light was rebuilt after a fire in 1776 and fitted with a reflector, and oil lamps instead of an open brazier. It was a great improvement; seamen had been sometimes obliged to awaken the old keeper at the earlier lighthouse with a shot to remind him that his fire needed blowing.

The annual gross profits of these lighthouses for 1823-5 were £458, and in 1837 Trinity House, under act of parliament, purchased the remaining rights from the owner, Frederick Lane. In 1844 the two old structures were demolished and a new lighthouse erected. Designed by James Walker, it was a circular tower of brick 61ft in height with a light 109ft above sea level. It was closed in 1922 and sold for £1,300. During World War II it was used as an artillery observation post and is now a private dwelling, visible from the cliff car park. Much of its former glory was lost with the demolition of one of the keepers' cottages and the removal of the lantern.

INNER DOWSING

Lightships were stationed at this Lincolnshire site in 1873, anchored in about ten fathoms of water near the north-east end of the shoal, and remained until Trinity House took an unusual opportunity to replace them in 1969. The National Coal Board, exploring seabed coal seams, used a large drilling platform built for them by the Cleveland Bridge and Engineering Company. The 230ft platform, when first built was the largest of its kind in the world, was used for locating and sampling coal seams, and was offered for sale when it became redundant. Trinity House bought it for £30,000.

Structural tests were carried out and proved positive but extensive alterations were necessary before it could be brought into operation as a lighthouse. The work was carried out at West Hartlepool where the structure was strengthened, converted and fitted out. Light, fog signal and ancillary equipment were installed and the accommodation (for the three keepers) modernised.

The cabin roof forms a landing platform for a helicopter and

*Inner Dowsing: the metal structure, commissioned in 1971, replaced a
lightship*

provides space for large storage tanks for oil, water and compressed
air.

In September 1971 the tower was towed from West Hartlepool
110 miles to its site on the shoal 14 miles north-east of Skegness.
It floated on buoyancy tanks, and when it reached the site was sunk
into position. The light was commissioned on 13 September 1971
and the last of the lightvessels towed away. The tower weighs 650
tons and stands in 50ft of water at low tide.

Established 1971
Height of light above MHW 142ft
Height of tower 212ft
Range 24 miles
W F (5sec), 580,000cp
Optic multicatoptric
Electricity, 240V 2.25W
Diaphone fog signal (60sec)
No public access

SPURN HEAD

The Humber estuary has always been difficult to navigate because of sandbanks which constantly change their shape and position, but dredgers keep a deep channel clear and marked for shipping. The important navigation lights are Spurn Head, Killingholme and Thorngumbald, although there is still an attractive unused tower in the village of Paull. The peninsula is a narrow tract of sand and shingle on which little grows except coarse grass, and is exposed to the gales of the North Sea.

Spurn Head: the tower (centre) seen across the Humber estuary and (right) in more detail

It is claimed that Spurn has the distinction of being Britain's first lighthouse, for in 1428 a hermit, Richard Reedbarrow, living at Ravenspurne, voluntarily erected a warning structure. He had seen so many lives, ships and goods lost on the headland that he devoted himself to building a tower that would be a beacon by day and a light by night. In 1428 he appealed to Henry VI's parliament at Leicester for help in erecting the lighthouse, and a grant was made giving him the right to impose a tax of twelvepence on vessels of 120 tons and upwards coming into the Humber, eightpence for vessels of 100 tons and fourpence for smaller ones. He was a man 'having compassion and pitee of the Christen people that ofte tymes are there perished'. Later, beacon and hermitage were engulfed by the sea, and further attempts to erect a lighthouse were always opposed, either by the local sailors who feared that the constantly changing channels could never be safely lit or by Trinity House who believed that a light would be to the advantage of an enemy.

Several Hull shipowners approached Justinian Angel, owner of the land at Spurn, in 1672, asking him to build a lighthouse. They promised to pay dues on a voluntary basis, but a charter was obtained from Charles II granting compulsory dues of one farthing a ton. The arrangement was an immediate success, and in 1678 it was decided to erect a second tower or low light and impose a tax of one halfpenny per ton on cargo. The new rear light was an octagonal tower 60ft high, the front was a ground level platform. Trinity House complained of Mr Angel's profits and some interesting facts came to light in his reply. He pointed out that the grate of a lighthouse was usually fastened to some sort of a back plate and exposed only on one side to the wind, but at Spurn it was necessary to show the light all round and it was therefore entirely unscreened. It was built on a swape (presumably a raised grate) 14ft above the top of the tower and burnt a vast amount of best coal. Repair costs were exceptional, for in such an exposed position the heat was so intense that it melted the iron bars of the grate (as many as four in one night). The Newcastle tenders offloaded their cargo some distance from the lights and the coal had to be carried over soft sand, into which the cartwheels sank, and then over sharp shingle which lamed many of the oxen. Keepers' salaries were heavy, for two men and a competent overseer were always on duty and on rough nights even more were needed.

Altogether, from the first lighting of the fires in November 1675 to Christmas 1677 the expenditure amounted to £905 and the receipts to £948, a slender £43 profit for two years' work.

As time passed, deposits of sand built up the point so much that the lights became deceptive and actually caused many wrecks. An act was passed in 1766 for 'taking down, and removing certain

Spurn Head: the light in 1773

lighthouses now standing near the Spurn Point at the mouth of the
Humber and for erecting other fit and convenient lighthouses instead
thereof'. John Smeaton, builder of one of the Eddystone lighthouses undertook to build a tower of 90ft and another of 50ft,
each with an enclosed lantern for the fire. The site chosen was
nearly a mile from the old towers, and the lower light was to be a
temporary structure. The station, completed in 1775, suffered in
January 1776 when a great storm washed away entirely the site of
the lower light, but the high light stood for over a century. The
lower light was again destroyed by a storm in 1786, 1787, 1816
and 1830.

The present lighthouse is a brick structure painted black with a
broad white band and white lantern. It stands at the head of the
peninsula, now a bird sanctuary, and is difficult to reach. Pleasure
trips from Grimsby once took visitors to within half a mile of the
point, but operate no longer.

Established 1775 (present tower 1895)
Height of light above MHW 120ft
Height of tower 128ft
Range 17 miles
W Fl (15sec), 138,000cp
Optic 3rd order catadioptric
Acetylene
No public access (unwatched)

HUMBER ESTUARY
(KILLINGHOLME AND THORNGUMBALD CLOUGH)

The village of Killingholme, not far from Grimsby, is now over-shadowed by the storage tanks of an oil refinery, but it was not many years ago that the lighthouses were a major feature of a landscape since marked by industrial development.

There are three towers: the high light, 78ft, was established in 1831 and rebuilt in 1876; the south low light, 45ft, was established

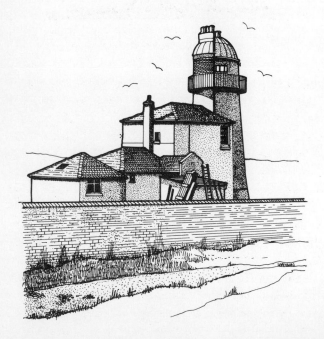

Humber Estuary: the old Killingholme north low light, now a private house

in 1836; the north low light and cottages were built in 1851 and became redundant in 1920.

The high light (W Occ, 9sec) has a range of 14 miles. The south low light (F W) has a range of 11 miles. Together, they lead shipping through the main channel into and from the Humber.

The north low light was used as a signal station for trawlers until a coastguard station was built nearby, and is now a private house.

Thorngumbald lights were established in 1870 to lead shipping between the village of Paull and the Hebbles; both show W Occ (2sec). The high light, a red-painted openwork iron structure, has a 9-mile range. The low light, white-painted, has a range of 8 miles. Originally, one of the towers could be moved to establish a new line for approaching vessels to follow.

The tower of the old lighthouse at Paull can be seen in the centre of the village.

WITHERNSEA

Withernsea lies between Spurn Head and Flamborough Head. Fine beaches stretch along this coastline and only beyond Bridlington do the sandstone cliffs of Flamborough start to dominate. Those who like fresh air and a brisk walk may take the footpath which follows the coast from Hornsea to Great Cowden and thence to Withernsea, a distance of about fifteen miles.

The lighthouse was built by Trinity House, and in conjunction with the Humber lightship keeps ships clear of Bridlington Bay and assists the passage to and from the Humber estuary. The tapering octagonal tower with lantern and cupola stands within the town, not far from the church and close to a school, shops and rows of terraced houses. The keeper's dwelling is set to one side of the tower and stands out from its brick-built neighbours because it is painted white.

This is a man-and-wife station and has a relief keeper.

Established 1894
Height of light above MHW 120ft
Height of tower 127ft
Range 17 miles
W Fl (3sec), 800,000cp

Optic 3rd order catadioptric
Electricity, 100V 1,500W
Open to public

Withernsea: the tall tapering tower is architecturally unusual in Britain

FLAMBOROUGH

An unlighted seamark has stood at Flamborough since 1669, built
by Sir John Clayton as a lighthouse but never kindled.

Flamborough Head's 200ft cliffs are a landfall for seamen in this
busy part of the North Sea and must have been familiar to the
fishing fleets, and the coasters plying between Hull and Dundee.

Flamborough: the imposing tower stands a few hundred yards from the extremity of Flamborough Head

The steamship *Forfarshire* struggled through these waters before being wrecked in sight of the Longstone light further north.

The present stone tower is one of the most magnificent of British lighthouses. Designed by the architect Samuel Wyatt, it is of elegant proportions, with an upper and lower gallery; the tower and its adjoining buildings are painted white. It was built by John Matson of Bridlington, who completed the work in nine months without, it is said, using scaffolding, at a cost of £8,000.

Established 1806
Height of light above MHW 214ft
Height of tower 87ft
Range 21.2 miles
W Gp Fl (15sec), 750,000cp
Optic 1st order catadioptric

Electricity, 100V 500W
Diaphone fog signals (90sec) 2 blasts
Open to public

SCARBOROUGH

Scarborough lighthouse is not in the same league of magnificence
as Flamborough; it is a local harbour beacon but nevertheless an
attraction in a holiday resort. It was built in 1806 at the end of
Vincent's Pier and flashed white or orange according to the depth
of water at the pier end; it replaced an iron basket in which wood
or coal was burned.

The present tower, of white-painted stone, is 64ft high and the
light (W Occ, 5sec) is 56ft above high water. A fixed orange light
is shown from a window in the same tower when there is less than
12ft of water over the bar. A diaphone fog signal (60sec) is installed.

The predecessor of the present tower was destroyed during
World War I when German gunboats came close inshore and
bombarded the town.

Scarborough: the station is the focal point of the small harbour

Whitby: the tower on Ling Hill, overlooking the harbour

WHITBY

High cliffs and fine beaches extend to Ravenscar around Robin Hood's Bay from Whitby and the area is popular with holiday-makers. Whitby is a seaside resort; its harbour is the base for the town's fishing fleet and it was from here that Captain Cook set out in the *Endeavour* on his voyage of discovery to Australia in 1768.

The harbour piers and their lights were built in 1831. The East Pier tower, a yellow-painted 43ft fluted column, shows fixed green and red lights; the West Pier tower, 73ft, shows a fixed green light. The green lights are exhibited when there is sufficient depth of water over the sand bar at the harbour entrance for vessels to enter. The red light shines over Whitby Rock. When the piers were extended, an extra light was placed on each pierhead (east, F R; west, F G).

Trinity House built the present tower on Ling Hill to the design of James Walker; originally a pair of towers, aligned north-south and showing fixed lights over Whitby Rock, the station was altered in 1890 when a more efficient light was installed in the smaller tower and the other closed down.

The fog signal is housed about 300yd from the present lighthouse.

Established 1858
Height of light above MHW 240ft
Height of tower 44ft
Range 22.1 miles
W R Occ (15sec), 57,000cp
Optic 1st order catadioptric
Paraffin vapour
Fog sirens (90sec) 4 blasts
Open to public

ROKER PIER, SUNDERLAND

The lighthouse at the head of Roker Pier, Sunderland, was completed in 1903. It is a white masonry tower with three red bands and a single-flashing light which shows every 5sec. It is about 80ft above high water and has a range of 15 miles.

The apparatus originally consisted of a gas burner but was soon replaced by a petroleum vapour burner in a large optic rotated by a hand-wound weight-driven clock. This increased the intensity of the light by about three times. The fog signal, a siren supplied with air from a gas-driven compressor, was regulated by a separate clock, automatically rewound every half hour by a small motor.

The light source was changed again in 1930, and since then this station, which is essentially automatic, has been the base for experimental and development work with automatic lamp changers and time switches.

SOUTER POINT

Souter Point, sometimes called Lizard Point, is midway between South Shields and Sunderland, and was the scene of great activity in the late 1860s and early '70s when Trinity House built the lighthouse station, keepers' dwellings and service roads. The present tower is white with a red band and lantern.

Following experiments at South Foreland and the successful electrification at Dungeness, Trinity House decided on electric power for Souter Point, and two new alternating current generators developed by Professor Holmes were installed (one is now in the Science Museum, London). Modernisation was carried out in 1947, and the need for a light of increased power was met by a 4½-ton biform optic.

Established 1871
Height of light above MHW 150ft
Height of tower 76ft
Range 18.4 miles
R Fl (5sec), 1,380,000cp
Optic 1st order biform catadioptric
Electricity, 100V 4,500W
Diaphone fog signals (30sec)
Open to public

RIVER TYNE

This important river, with its shipyards, docks, wharves and factories, was one of the earliest to have a seamark. Two towers were built at North Shields c1540, and a coal-fired light was established at Tynemouth Castle c1550. During the sixteenth century, coal boats in great numbers started to ply between the Tyne and London, and shipmasters petitioned the king for coastal lights. Henry VIII responded by granting a charter to Trinity House of Newcastle in 1536 for the building of lighthouses from Blyth to Whitby and the collection of dues for upkeep.

The towers at North Shields had one candle in each, and when kept in line marked the navigable channel. The number of candles was increased to two in 1613 and to three in 1727 when the towers were rebuilt. Nine years later copper reflectors were installed, and in 1773 oil lamps replaced the candles. The present square towers, with white lanterns and seaward faces, were built in 1808. They are 60ft in height and both show a fixed white light with a range of 20 miles. The present optics were installed about 1902.

The fire at Tynemouth Castle was coal-burning, and as it was sited near the coalfield of Northumberland there was never any question of shortage of fuel. It was established by Crown patent and remained in private hands until 1836. Trinity House of Newcastle, responding to complaints about the state of the light, tried to get the patent cancelled at the end of the seventeenth century. They failed, and it was not until empowered by act of parliament in 1836 that Trinity House of London took it over and paid compensation of £124,678 to the owner.

The present light is a masonry tower 75ft high on the North Pier head (Gp Fl W (10sec), 26 miles); the fog signal, a horn type, is on the cupola. The South Pier head tower, 41ft (W R G Occ (10sec), 13.6 (G 8) miles) has a bell fog signal.

Both lights date from the late 1800s and, like all others on the river Tyne, are maintained by the Port of Tyne authority.

St Mary's Island: visitors must cross the causeway at low tide

ST MARY'S ISLAND

St Mary's Island, sometimes called Bait Island, is linked to Whitley Bay by a causeway which is flooded at high tide. The relative accessibility of the lighthouse and its pleasant surroundings make it popular with visitors.

Established 1898
Height of light above MHW 120ft
Height of tower 120ft
Range 17 miles

W Gp Fl (20sec), 523,000cp
Optic 1st order catadioptric
Paraffin vapour
Open to public

BLYTH

Blyth is three miles north of Whitley Bay. It is an industrial town, its development dating from the seventeenth century and the expanding coal industry, and has a deep harbour which was linked by rail to Bebside colliery. The high light, built in 1788 to a design of Sir Matthew White Ridley, was a round tower 40ft high lit by oil lamps. An attendant, one of the Blyth pilots, was appointed to keep the station.

Gas replaced oil in 1857 and the following year the height of the tower was increased by 14ft; alterations in 1900 brought it to its present height. The tower, a leading light and one of a group of Blyth Harbour lights, stands about 250yd from the front tower; both show F G, range 12 miles. In 1932, when the installation was electrified, the town gas supply remained as stand-by.

COQUET ISLAND

The island is a low tract of pastureland lying close inshore off the Northumberland coast; the substantial lighthouse on the south-west shore was built by Trinity House to James Walker's design. Dwelling houses are an integral part of the fortress-like rock station.

Established 1841
Height of light above MHW 83ft
Height of tower 72ft
Range 14.9 miles
W R Occ (30sec), 59,000cp
Optic 1st order catadioptric
Paraffin vapour
Explosive fog signal (3 mins)
No public access

BAMBURGH

Trinity House built the black-painted circular lighthouse, supported on piles, at Black Rock Point near Bamburgh in Northumberland and the station was electrified in 1967.

Grace Darling was born in Bamburgh and the town has a small museum with exhibits from the Longstone lighthouse, where her father was principal keeper.

Established 1910
Height of light above MHW 44ft
Height of tower 36ft
Range 12 miles
W R G Gp Occ (15sec), 27,000cp
Optic 3rd order dioptric
Electricity, 50V 500W
No public access (unwatched)

FARNE ISLANDS

This group of islands takes its name from Farne, the largest and closest to the mainland of the Northumberland coast. Sites such as

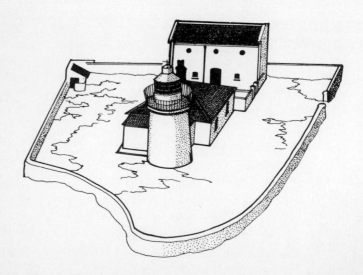

Farne Islands: this compact clifftop station has been unmanned since 1966

this, safe yet not remote, were strongholds of the early Christian church, and St Cuthbert lived alone in a cell on Farne from 675-85. The islands are in two distinct groups separated by Staples Sound, and by their position in the main deepwater coastal lanes present a hazard to shipping.

Sir John Clayton erected a tower on the Farne Islands as part of his comprehensive scheme for the east coast, but the influential Newcastle merchants refused to pay him dues for its upkeep and no fire was kindled. Proposals were made in 1727 by coastal traders in the area, but there was no action for fifty years until, in July 1776, Trinity House took out a patent to erect two lighthouses, one on Farne and the other on Staples Island.

The Staples Island light station consisted of a stone cottage with its roof sloping up to a central glazed lantern, and it is most likely that oil lamps were used. It was closed down in 1826 when Trinity House erected the lighthouse on the outer Longstone Rock.

The Farne light, sited on the south-west point of the island, had a coal-fire at the top of the tower. It was a cause of discontent among shipowners because it was badly kept. The Blackett family, who owned the islands and held the lease, were compelled by Trinity House to install reflectors which they did in 1800, receiving a new patent which gave them an increased income. Trinity House later took over the patent.

The present lighthouse, built in 1811, was designed by Daniel Alexander. A smaller tower was built at the same time, about 200yd distant from the main lighthouse, but was closed down early this century.

Established 1776
Height of light above MHW 87ft
Height of tower 43ft
Range 15.2 miles
W R Gp Fl (15sec), 4,400,000cp
Optic 3rd order catadioptric
Acetylene
No public access (unwatched)

LONGSTONE

By the early nineteenth century the need had become clear for a light on the Longstone Rock, about six miles offshore in the region of the Farne Islands. The Longstone lighthouse, built to the design of Joseph Nelson, was first lit in February 1826.

The station is bleak and the isolation must have been at times hard to bear for its most famous inhabitant, Grace Darling, daughter of William, the principal keeper. Conditions were sometimes so violent that the family had to take refuge in the upper part of the tower from enormous waves that battered their living quarters.

Longstone: Grace Darling's father was principal keeper here; the illustration shows the light as it was before modernisation in 1952

Grace was twenty-two when the *Forfarshire*, out of Hull with a cargo and sixty-four passengers and crew for Dundee in September 1838, was driven hard on to the Big Harcar Rocks less than half a mile from the lighthouse and broke in two. The stern was swept away but the forepart remained on the rocks. Early the following morning Grace glanced from her window and saw the wreck with

116

survivors clinging to it. Rousing her father, she insisted on attempting a rescue. They reached the ship and took off four men and a woman, returning with one of the men as volunteer to save the remaining four people.

News of the feat reached the newspapers and Grace Darling became a national heroine. She lived only four more years and died of tuberculosis on 20 October 1842.

Major alterations to the lighthouse were carried out in 1952, when electricity was laid on and the optic and fog signal apparatus renewed. The Trinity House boat that services the station is aptly named *Grace Darling*.

> Established 1826
> Height of light above MHW 75ft
> Height of tower 85ft
> Range 14.4 miles
> W Fl (20sec), 3,200,000cp
> Optic small 3rd order catadioptric
> Electricity, 100V 1,000W
> Fog siren (60sec) 2 blasts
> No public access

THE WEST COAST
AND THE ISLE OF MAN

The Isle of Man (Map D p 30)

St Bees Head to Strumble Head (Map D p 30)

South Bishop to Pendeen (Map A p 28)

THE ISLE OF MAN

The Isle of Man lies more or less centrally in the Irish Sea and has a rugged coastline which must have been a serious danger to vessels. The loss of life and property at the turn of the eighteenth century caused great concern among the pilot committee of the port of Liverpool and as early as 1658 it is recorded that a scheme to put a light on the Calf of Man was supported by the mariners of Chester, Liverpool and other ports in the north and west. It was opposed by Trinity House who maintained that the dues would be a burden to shipowners.

During a meeting in 1771 the pilots discussed the establishment of a light on either Langness or the Calf of Man, the latter being favoured. It was suggested that two leading lights should be built to guide shipping past Langness Point and other dangers to the south of the island, particularly the Chicken Rock. Robert Stevenson visited the site in 1801 and discussed the proposed lighthouses with the receiver-general of the customs, noting that no provision for lighthouses on the Isle of Man had been made in any act of parliament, and recording it as desirable to have the island included in the next act referring to the northern lighthouses. Thus it was that the northern lighthouse commissioners, instead of Trinity House took responsibility for the Isle of Man.

Stevenson maintained that a small charge was necessary for the upkeep of a lighthouse on the Calf of Man, the vessels passing were so numerous, but each proposal by Trinity House was considered to be too high by the merchants of Liverpool.

CALF OF MAN

Robert Stevenson produced his designs for two leading lighthouses for the Calf of Man in 1816; he considered that this was 'one of the most necessary situations in Great Britain'. Work began in February

1818 and Stevenson visited the site in August: '. . . the work was found a credit to inspector and contractors, but proceeding too slowly'. The station, situated on the cliffs at the south end of the Calf of Man, comprised two towers on sites 560ft apart aligned to indicate a safer course past the low-lying Chicken Rock. The lanterns, 375ft and 282ft above sea level, held 'double-revolving and leading lights without colour' with a range of 6 to 7 leagues.

The towers were discontinued in 1875 when a sea tower was constructed on the Chicken Rock.

Following a serious fire at Chicken Rock in 1962, the Northern Lighthouse Board built a new station on the Calf of Man in preference to re-equipping Chicken Rock. It is sited near the old low light tower. The concrete 8-sided tower rises from a granite building on this imposing site; the fog signal is located to the south of the tower.

> Established 1818 (present station 1968)
> Height of light above MHW 306ft
> Height of tower 35ft
> Range 24 miles
> W Fl (15sec), 2,000,000cp
> Optic 16 sealed beam units
> Electricity, 30V 3,200W
> Electric fog horn (45sec)
> Open to public

POINT OF AYRE

The lighthouse, situated on a sandy common about a quarter of a mile from the sea, was designed by Robert Stevenson. He visited the site when the building was under way in 1818 and recorded: '. . . arrived at the Point of Ayre, where . . . a lighthouse was being built. In consequence of faulty workmanship the inspector was given notice to leave . . . with a month's pay'.

A second tower, established in 1891, stands close to high water mark at the extremity of the point. It is 34ft high and shows W Fl (3sec) with an 8-mile range; it houses a fog siren (90sec) 3 blasts.

Point of Ayre: the station is sited among sand dunes and is popular with tourists

Established 1819
Height of light above MHW 106ft
Height of tower 99ft
Range 19 miles
W R Alt Fl (60sec), 66,000cp
Optic 1st order catadioptric
Paraffin vapour
Open to public

CHICKEN ROCK

The lighthouses at the Calf of Man were often shrouded in fog, and thus of little use to shipping attempting to steer a safe course past the Chicken Rock, islets about one mile south of the Calf of Man and exposed to the full force of the sea. At high water the rocks are covered to a depth of five or six feet.

In 1869 the commissioners for northern lighthouses determined to mark the Chicken Rock with a first-class rock light. They called in the Stevenson family of engineers, at that time represented by David and Thomas who had already experienced work on rock

123

towers with their father, Alan, and grandfather Robert. The two brothers designed a strong and graceful tower the shape of which was based on a hyperbolic curve. Teams of masons were employed and housed at Port St Mary, a small fishing village about four miles from the rock. Workshops were built, the granite ordered, and steam tug engaged to carry men and supplies to the site. The tug carried two small boats from which landings were made on the rock itself; the tug could not approach too closely. All men were compelled to wear life jackets at all times, and not one life was lost in the five seasons of work. Work was regulated by the state of tide and weather, sometimes six or seven hours being possible at a stretch and others only one or two. When the weather was really bad, work on site was not possible, and the season ended in September. The 35-man gang carried on during the closed season, preparing the granite for the following year's work. Each piece was cut, dove-tailed, numbered and a template made in case of accidental loss

Chicken Rock: a beautifully proportioned sea tower built by David and Thomas Stevenson

or damage. Each course was laid out in the yard so that the stones could be checked before being dispatched

The site was prepared during 1870 and nine complete courses were set in place. The following season, a further fourteen courses were laid to complete the solid base. Work progressed quickly in 1872, when another forty-seven courses were completed and the topmost course, the ninety-sixth, was laid on 6 June 1873. The interior was fitted out, furnished and the lantern and optic installed the following year. In all, 3,557 tons of granite were dressed and fixed in place. The tower's eight floors contained store rooms, kitchen, two bedrooms and the light room. The total cost was £64,559.

The optic, designed by Thomas Stevenson and described as a dioptric holophotal system, was an 8-sided frame with large annular lenses on each face. It revolved around the oil vapour burner once every four minutes, giving an intense light of 43,000 candlepower. The characteristic was changed when the apparatus was modernised. Two fog bells suspended from the lantern gallery were supplemented about 1890 by an explosive fog signal.

The lighthouse was gutted by fire in 1962 and its major function taken over by a new station on the Calf of Man. Chicken Rock was made automatic.

> Established 1875
> Height of light above MHW 123ft
> Height of tower 143ft
> Range 13 miles
> W Fl (5sec), 46,000cp
> Optic small 4th order catadioptric
> Propane gas
> Fog signal, battery-operated (60sec)
> No public access (unwatched)

LANGNESS

This station, more primitive in style than the other Manx lights, is an important establishment in an area where fog is common. It is situated at Dreswick Point, on the eastern side of Langness

Established 1880
Height of light above MHW 76ft
Height of tower 63ft
Range 21 miles
W Gp Fl (30sec), 200,000cp
Optic 2nd order catadioptric
Petroleum vapour
Siren fog signal 2 blasts
Open to public

Langness Point: this light lacks the graceful lines of its near-contemporary at Douglas Head

DOUGLAS HEAD

The northern lighthouse commissioners established this station to mark the entrance to Douglas Bay and to augment navigational aids in a busy seaway. The white stone tower, designed by David and Thomas Stevenson who followed their father, Alan, as engineers to the commissioners, stands in a courtyard surrounded by service rooms and keepers' dwellings. The buildings are flat-roofed and castellated, typifying a style favoured by this Scottish family of engineers and designers.

This lighthouse is perhaps the most-visited in the Isle of Man; the views from the lantern are magnificent and range from the English Lake District to the mountains of North Wales.

Established 1832
Height of light above MHW 104ft
Height of tower 65ft
Range 20 miles
W Gp QFl (30sec), 89,500cp
Optic 4th order catadioptric
Paraffin vapour
Diaphone fog signal (20sec)
Open to public

DOUGLAS HARBOUR LIGHT

This structure of 'polished ashlar erected upon the head of the famous pier in 1796' is now white-painted with a red band. The original light in the 35ft tower, four Argand burners with parabolic

Douglas Head: the view from the lantern makes this one of the Isle of Man's most-visited lighthouses

reflectors, was so efficient that only two burners were required at one time. The optic was improved further in 1897 and now shows W R Alt (15sec) with a 5-mile range. In fog, a bell sounds every 2sec.

MAUGHOLD HEAD

Until 1914, ships crossing the Irish Sea between Belfast and Douglas were without a seamark for 24 miles once Point of Ayre was passed. Their next landfall was Douglas Head. Maughold Head, a large headland, obscured this lighthouse and the danger from lack of a navigational aid in foggy conditions, which are common in the area of the Isle of Man, was considerable. A light was therefore established at Maughold Head and sited halfway down the slope

Maughold Head: a fine example of twentieth-century construction (1914) and a favourite with visitors because of its beautiful situation

of the headland to keep it below the level of the mist belt.
The sturdy round tower has two galleries.

Established 1914
Height of light above MHW 212ft
Height of tower 77ft
Range 22 miles
W Gp Fl (30sec), 569,000cp
Optic 1st order catadioptric
Paraffin vapour
Fog siren (90sec)
Open to public

ST BEES HEAD

South of the harbours of Maryport, Workington and Whitehaven sandy beaches and grassy foreshores give way to cliffs around St Bees Head, a high promontory, which was a danger to small coastal vessels trading between the ports of Wales and the Solway Firth. In the early eighteenth century there were no lights to guide shipping in these waters. In 1718, Trinity House obtained a patent for the building of a lighthouse on the Head and in turn leased it to a private individual, Thomas Lutwige, for ninety-nine years at an annual rent of £20. Lutwige undertook to erect the tower and maintain a light at his own expense; to provide him with an income, dues were levied at a rate of three-halfpence a ton on cargo of vessels calling at nearby ports.

Lutwige built a strong round tower 30ft in height and 16ft in diameter, probably of local sandstone, on top of which was a large metal grate into which the keepers tipped loads of coal. To help them avoid the stifling smoke as they climbed, ladders were placed round the tower at intervals and they would use those which the wind kept clear. Work was strenuous, particularly on windy nights, and the keepers were rewarded with a weekly wage of seven shillings.

The lighthouse was visited by Robert Stevenson on the first of his English tours in 1801, and he described the site thus:

St Bees Head light is from coals exposed upon the top of an old tower in an open chauffer, which is at top only two feet diameter, at bottom one foot six inches and two feet deep; so that in storms so small a body of fire cannot be kept up as it ought to be. About one hundred and thirty tons of coal are said to be used annually.

130

The small grate led to continual complaints from shipowners because on windy nights the light was variable in intensity and often shrouded in thick smoke.

St Bees Head: the present tower replaced the last coal-fired light in Britain in 1822

In 1822, the tower was destroyed by fire and Trinity House decided to substitute oil lights for coal (St Bees was the last coal-fired lighthouse in Britain); to replace the old tower a fine circular lighthouse was built to the design of Joseph Nelson. This tower, which cost £2,322, is the one in use today. The present optic and fog signals date from 1951.

> Established 1718 (present tower 1822)
> Height of light above MHW 336ft
> Height of tower 55ft
> Range 25.4 miles
> W Gp Occ (20sec), 146,000cp
> Optic 1st order catadioptric
> Electricity, 240V 1,500W
> Electric fog horns (45sec) 2 blasts
> Open to public

ISLE OF WALNEY

Walney Island is a spit of land about fourteen miles long and less than a mile in width, separated by a narrow stretch of water from the mainland at Barrow-in-Furness. To the south-east it forms a natural wall to the harbour, the base of several local sailing clubs. The lighthouse stands at the entrance to Morecambe Bay, which is so shallow that it is possible to walk across it at certain stages of the tide. The deepwater channels of the bay are indicated by leading lights.

The merchants of Lancaster were successful in their petition of 1789 to mark the sands of Morecambe Bay, and were granted leave to build a lighthouse on the Isle of Walney and to collect dues from vessels using the neighbouring ports. A tower was built in 1790 and an oil light with a parabolic reflector was first shown on 1 December of that year. The light was improved in 1791 when Richard Walker installed his new revolving apparatus which gave a flashing light, distinct from the fixed lights at St Bees and Liverpool. He charged just over £21. Robert Stevenson visited the station in 1801 and made a note of the apparatus, an arrangement of three 3ft parabolic reflectors fixed back to back around a central axis. A motor driven by a weight revolved the

Isle of Walney: this tower, with its unique optic, stands in a nature reserve off Barrow in Furness

apparatus once every fifteen minutes and the Argand lamps
produced one long flash every five minutes. The reflectors were
made from 721 small pieces of mirror glass bedded in plaster of
Paris on a wooden frame. Two keepers maintained the light.

In December 1803 the lantern caught fire and was destroyed.
The present stone octagonal tower was started the following year.
The light was changed in 1820 when four silver-plated copper re-
flectors with Argand burners were installed, designed by Robert
Stevenson; although the light source has changed, the optic is
still in use. The apparatus is now unique in English lighthouses.
The reflectors, normally kept covered during daylight hours, are
not the originals, one of which is in Lancaster museum

The weight-driven motor for turning the optic was replaced by
an electric motor in 1956.

The lighthouse service has a tradition of long-serving families
(a descendant of Henry Knott, keeper at one of the Foreland
lights in 1730, retired in 1910) and the Swarbrick family
have been associated with Walney for over eighty years. An assistant
at the time of writing, Peg Swarbrick came to Walney as a small girl
when her father was appointed assistant. Her sister Ella held the
position until 1967 and Peg, now Mrs Braithwaite, took over.

The Isle of Walney lighthouse is owned by the Port of Lancaster
Commission and stands in a nature reserve which cannot be visited
without permission.

> Established 1790
> Height of light above MHW 66ft
> Height of tower 80ft
> Range 23 miles
> W Fl (15sec)
> Electricity
> No public access

FLEETWOOD

A navigable channel between the sandbanks of Morecambe Bay is
marked by a set of leading lights at Fleetwood, at the entrance to the
river Wyre. The low light stands on the esplanade and the high light
is about 300yds from it; only the low light is in use today, and
although the original light still stands its function has been taken
over by a 13ft tower showing a fixed white light.

The low light was established in the early 1840s; it is about 40ft high and shows W F, range 8 miles. The designer was Decimus Burton.

The channel is marked on the north-east extremity of North Wharf sandbank by a 31ft screw pile lighthouse dating from 1840. It was rammed and carried away by the schooner *Elizabeth and Jane* of Preston in 1870, but was re-erected and the colour changed to black to make it more conspicuous. The light shows W R Fl (15sec) and there is a fog bell (30sec).

RIVER MERSEY

A perch marker (a pole serving as an aid to navigation) on a group of rocks at the mouth of the Mersey was so frequently destroyed by shipping in the late eighteenth and early nineteenth centuries that Lieut Evans, a Royal Navy surveyor, suggested as early as 1812 that a permanent light should be built. A Mersey pilot boat collided with the perch in stormy weather in 1821, an accident which set in motion the procedures leading to the establishment of a light.

The dock trustees were petitioned to replace the perch but deliberation and delay accounted for six years until, in June 1827, the construction of Rock lighthouse was started. The light first showed in March 1830 and was altered in 1878 to W Fl (20sec) with a range of 14 miles from 77ft above sea level.

The granite tower is 89ft high and was originally equipped with two fog bells of different tones; they are no longer used.

POINT OF AIR (Disused)

In common with the Humber and Morecambe Bay, the estuaries of the Dee and Mersey suffer from the deposition of sand and the constantly changing shape of the sea bed, necessitating regular dredging of deepwater channels.

The Liverpool Pilotage Service undertook to provide an efficient lighthouse system and built three towers in 1763, one at Hoylake and two at Leasowe. A press report of 1782 notes: 'Some evil disposed person wilfully broke seven panes in the lower light of the wooden lighthouse at Hoylake with stones.'

Another lighthouse was built at Bidston Hill in 1771 and others at Formby and Crosby, but most were eventually replaced by lightships and buoys. The tower at New Brighton was an exception.

Point of Air: a lightship took over the functions of this tower nearly a century ago; the tower has not been used since then

The Point of Air light was established in 1776 according to Trinity House and 1777 according to a local press report, which stated that the tower was completed and would show two lights, one to seaward towards Great Ormes Head (Llandudno) and the other towards Dawpool, Cheshire. The tower still stands, and fifty or so yards to the east a stone bearing the initials TH — presumably Trinity House — is bedded in the sand. Originally red and white-striped with a red lantern, the tower is now white; it showed two lights, one 63ft and one 8ft above sea level. Trinity House built this local light for the benefit of Liverpool and Chester and leased it to Chester County Council.

The Dee lightship was established in December 1883 and the Point of Air lighthouse closed down.

GREAT ORMES HEAD

The lighthouse is situated on the headland not far from Llandudno and is familiar to countless holidaymakers, many of whom may at first not recognise the fortress-like building for what it is. The short tower is not visible from the approach road. The height above sea level is such that there is no need for a tall building.

135

Great Ormes Head: the fortress-like station is essential to Liverpool's sea traffic

Great Ormes Head: the lantern room on the cliff edge

Before the lighthouse was built, no local navigational marks existed in spite of busy traffic to and from the Dee and Mersey ports. The Liverpool dock authorities took the initiative and started the procedures which led eventually to the establishment of the light. The Mersey Docks and Harbour Company maintained it until 1973 when it was handed over to Trinity House.

> Established 1862
> Height of light above MHW 325ft
> Height of tower 37ft
> Range 21 miles (W), 18 miles (R)
> W R Fl (30sec), 190,00 0cp (W), 46,000cp (R)
> Optic 1st order catadioptric
> (W flashes letter B in morse code)
> Electricity, 100V 1,000W
> Open to public

TRWYN-DU

The island of Anglesey, off the coast of North Wales, must be rounded by coastal shipping making the passage up or down the western seaboard, and as a consequence of its position in a busy seaway has several major lights. Skerries was built first, followed a century later by South Stack and then Point Lynas, the latter after the wreck of the *Rothesay Castle* on Puffin Island at the entrance to the Menai Strait about 1830.

The Liverpool master pilots had already been consulted about the advisability of a light on the shore at Black Point, or Trwyn-du, but no action was taken until late in the 1830s when Trinity House built the present station. It is sited on a low-lying rock surrounded by shingle beaches about half a mile south of Puffin Island, and the circular stone tower is distinguished by its three black bands. It is clearly visible from the mainland and the coast of Anglesey.

> Established 1838
> Height of light above MHW 61ft
> Height of tower 96ft
> Range 13.4 miles

W Fl (5.5sec), 15,000cp
Optic 1st order catadioptric
Acetylene
Fog bell (30sec)
No public access (unwatched)

POINT LYNAS

The visitor to this lighthouse must climb steeply up a narrow road, preferably on foot because there is no room for two vehicles to pass. The view from the top merits the climb.

The station, a low castellated structure, stands on the south coast of Anglesey and is fully automatic. Its history goes back to the eighteenth century when it was decided to establish a station where Liverpool-bound ships could pick up their pilots; this site was chosen by representatives of the Liverpool Pilotage Service, and early pilots used a farmhouse as a lookout post. Later, two oil lamps with reflectors were set in a tower, and this optic was used in the new lighthouse when it was commissioned.

Point Lynas: a dual-purpose establishment — lighthouse, and pilot station for the Mersey ports

The cost of building the station was £1,165, considerably less than the expense of modernisation, which took place in the 1960s.

The automatic fog detector brings the fog signal into operation when visibility drops below 2½ miles.

Trinity House assumed responsibility for Point Lynas in 1973.

> Established 1835
> Height of light above MHW 128ft
> Height of tower 37ft
> Range 20 miles
> W Occ (10sec), 112,000cp
> Electricity, 100V 1,000W
> Fog horn (45sec)
> Open to public

SKERRIES

The Skerries is a low tract of land, part of which is submerged to become an extensive shoal seven miles north-east of Holyhead and in the path of shipping Mersey-bound from the south. The first proposal to build a lighthouse here came in 1658 from Henry Hascard, a private speculator who appealed to Cromwell's Council of State but was strongly opposed by Trinity House and the appeal rejected. The next petition, put forward in 1705 with the backing of many Irish Sea traders, was again opposed by Trinity House who offered a counter-proposal that they should build a light for which the merchants should pay dues. The merchants refused and the matter lapsed.

It was not until 1714 that William Trench, the wealthy lease-holder of the Skerries, successfully gained a patent giving him the right to build a lighthouse and exact dues of one penny and two-pence a ton of cargo at a Crown rent of £5 a year.

Trench agreed to bear the initial cost, but the venture was marked by tragedy and disappointment. His son lost his life when the first shipload of materials was wrecked, and the work was not finished until 1717 when the lighthouse stood 'about 150ft higher than ye sea around it and on ye 4th of November a fire was kindled therein and ever since supported'. It was not supported, however. The traders evaded payment of dues and Trench died in 1729, a

139

Skerries: seven miles north east of Holyhead, this light marks a hazard to Mersey-bound ships

broken man. The lease passed to his daughter, who was forced to sell it for a nominal sum; the final irony was that as trade between Liverpool and America increased the Skerries became immensely profitable, to such an extent that when Trinity House bought the remainder of the lease in 1836 it cost them nearly £445,000.

The original tower, 36ft high, was surmounted by a grate that burned up to eighty tons of coal a year; the fire was replaced by an oil lamp in 1804 and the tower extended upwards 22ft. The present lighthouse, modernised in 1967, is white with a broad red band.

Established 1714
Height of light above MHW 119ft (W), 86ft (R)
Height of tower 75ft
Range 17 miles (W), 16 miles (R)
W Gp Fl (10sec), 4,000,000cp; R F 20,000cp
Optic 1st order catadioptric
Electricity, 100V 1,500W
Diaphone fog signal (60sec) 2 blasts
Open to public

SOUTH STACK

The coastline of Holyhead Island, off Anglesey, rises in cliffs over 200ft high towards the south-west. South Stack is a rock island about 100ft in height, separated from the cliff face by a wide chasm through which the sea surges with great force; the lighthouse is situated on the rock's plateau-like top and spectators can look down on it from the clifftop. To reach the rock, Trinity House workmen cut 400 steps in the cliff face to take them to rock level and from this point slung a rope bridge across the chasm, and a hemp cable along which a basket carrying supplies was pulled. The rope bridge was replaced by an iron suspension bridge in 1828.

South Stack: the archetypal station — white-walled, set on a rock; the light guides Irish Sea traffic to Holyhead

David Alexander designed the light for Trinity House, who proposed it, and three keepers were appointed at an annual salary of £60 and sixteen tons of free coal. The original lamps burned oil and were replaced first by paraffin vapour and then, in 1938, by electricity.

The most memorable day in the history of the lighthouse was 25 October 1859, when one of the worst gales of the century occurred and over 200 ships were driven ashore or totally lost together with 800 passengers and crew. Among them was the steamship *Royal Charter,* which foundered with the loss of 500 lives. In the evening, assistant keeper John Jones was crossing the bridge to the lighthouse when a falling rock struck him on the head. He managed to reach the island before collapsing, and the principal keeper found him next morning. He died three weeks later.

Established 1809
Height of light above MHW 197ft
Height of tower 91ft
Range 20.5 miles
W Fl (10sec), 2,500,000cp
Optic 1st order catadioptric
Electricity, 100V 3500W
Tannoy fog horns (30sec)
Open to public

HOLYHEAD HARBOUR

The busy harbour of Holyhead is protected by a breakwater which carries a square stone tower with a black band. It was built in 1873, is 63ft high and the light shows W Gp Fl (15sec) with a range of 14 miles.

A lighthouse dating from 1821 stands at the head of Admiralty Pier in the old harbour and shows a fixed red light with a 1-mile range to guide ships into harbour clear of shoal water. The tower is 48ft high.

BARDSEY ISLAND

The island, about two miles long and half a mile wide, is separated from the Lleyn peninsula (Llŷn in Welsh) by Bardsey Sound. Bardsey was a refuge for Celtic divines and scholars in the sixth century and like the Farne Islands it became a centre of early Christianity. By the time of the death in 612 of the patron of the

142

Bardsey Island: one of the few square light towers around Britain's coast

abbey, St Dolmers, it was known all over Britain and the remains of many venerable monks were carried there for burial.

The lighthouse, a massive square tower, stands at the island's southerly tip. It is the major landfall for shipping heading north across Cardigan Bay. The tower has been floodlit since 1973 to reduce the hazard to migrating birds

Established 1821
Height of light above MHW 129ft
Height of tower 99ft
Range 17.5 miles
W Gp Fl (15sec), 2,000,000cp
Optic 1st order catadioptric
Electricity, 100V 1,500W
Tannoy fog horns (45sec) Mo (N)
Open to public

ST TUDWAL'S

Bardsey lighthouse is obscured from some quarters and, to compensate for this, a station was opened on the island of St Tudwal's

off the Lleyn peninsula. The establishment is compact, with a
small round tower, and the light is automatic.

Established 1877
Height of light above MHW 151ft
Height of tower 35ft
Range 18.4 miles
W R Fl (20sec), 12,000cp
Optic 2nd order catadioptric
Acetylene
No public access (unwatched)

STRUMBLE HEAD

The lighthouse is approached by miles of narrow, twisting roads
between high banks, leading on to the headland; the setting is wild

Strumble Head: this remote Pembrokeshire station is open to visitors

and bleak in bad weather. The station is on an islet, connected to
the mainland by a footbridge and marks the entrance to Fishguard
Bay and the harbour. Like St Tudwal's, it is a compact station; its

position makes a high tower unnecessary. Its light is one of the most powerful around the British coast.

Tame rabbits, tortoises, gerbils and guinea pigs live in complete freedom on the islet.

Established 1908
Height of light above MHW 148ft
Height of tower 55ft
Range 18.4 miles
W Gp Fl (15sec), 6,000,000cp
Optic 1st order catadioptric
Electricity, 100V 3,500W
Fog horn (60sec)
Open to public

SOUTH BISHOP

Southbound shipping passes Strumble Head and picks up the South Bishop light which, like so many lighthouses on this coast, is set high on a rock. The station was designed by James Walker; the

South Bishop: perches around the lantern here were built for the benefit of migrating birds, which used to fly to their deaths against the glass

roofs of the keepers' houses slope in a way which is normal on land but unusual in a situation like this. The dwellings were apparently intended for two families but it is doubtful whether anyone other than the keepers lived on the rock, which is so exposed that the sea sometimes floods the courtyard and breaks low windows.

The keepers are relieved by helicopter, but before this service was instituted they had to land from a tender and climb steps cut into the sheer rock face.

The lighthouse was built in the path of migrating birds, thousands of which killed themselves when they flew into the glass panels of the lantern. Trinity House, in co-operation with the Royal Society for the Protection of Birds, erected perches on the lantern and the mortality rate has been reduced considerably.

> Established 1839
> Height of light above MHW 144ft
> Height of tower 36ft
> Range, 18.2 miles
> W Fl (5sec), 576,000cp
> Optic 4th order catadioptric
> Electricity, 100V, 1,000W
> Diaphone fog signals (45sec) 3 blasts
> No public access

SMALLS

The Smalls are a group of rocks lying in the entrance to St George's Channel. They are a particular danger to shipping because they never show more than a dozen feet above high tides and are exposed to Atlantic and Irish Sea currents. When the sea is rough, the rocks are completely submerged. John Phillips, a Liverpool Quaker, proposed to build a lighthouse here in 1774 as a 'great and holy good to serve and save humanity'. He chose the design of Henry Whiteside, a Liverpool musical instrument maker: an octagonal tower of oak 15ft in diameter, supported on nine cast iron piles spaced around a central oak pillar. The outer piles were 40ft in length and the tower rose to a height of 65ft. The adjoining house had two rooms, a living room below divided into compartments for sleeping berths and stores, and a lightroom and lantern above.

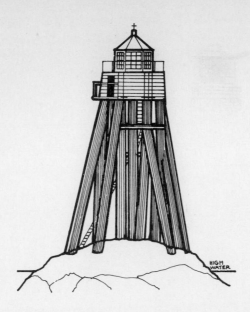

Smalls: the original wooden structure, which stood for eighty years

Whiteside hired a gang of miners and set out for the rock in June 1775 to survey the site and begin the foundation. They made their base at Solva, a small haven twenty-five miles from the Smalls. During their first landing the sea suddenly became rough and they were marooned. One of the iron piles had already been sunk into the rock and the men lashed themselves to it until rescued at the next low tide. Later, Whiteside saw that the pile had been damaged by the sea and substituted oak for the five main pillars. Before work was resumed, iron rings were fixed to the rock to which the workmen lashed themselves for safety.

The second season proved fruitful. Whiteside assembled his lighthouse temporarily at Solva and knew that each part would fit accurately when it reached the rock. Work began in the spring and by September the oil lamps were lit. The piles, though they stood for eighty years, looked insecure and in bad weather the whole structure trembled and swayed. The winter of 1776 was particularly bad and Whiteside had to set out for the Smalls with a repair gang; they were stranded there during severe storms. Whiteside, fearing the worst, wrote a note, put it in a bottle and tossed it into the sea:

147

Smalls: the present tower

The Smalls, February 1st 1777

Sir, — Being now in a most dangerous and distressed condition upon the Smalls, do hereby trust Providence will bring to your hand this, which prayeth for your immediate assistance to fetch us off the Smalls before the next spring (tide), or we fear we shall perish; our water near all gone, our fire quite gone, and our house in a most melancholy manner. I doubt not but you will fetch us from here as fast as possible; we can be got off at some part of the tide almost any weather. I need say no more, but remain your distressed humble servant.

H. Whiteside.

The men survived, but drastic repairs to the tower were needed and Phillips could not afford to carry them out. He therefore discharged the keepers and put out the light, making over his interest to a committee of Liverpool traders who in turn gave it to Trinity House. They rewarded Phillips by granting him a lease for 99 years at the rent of only £5 a year, and as it turned out this was reward indeed. When Trinity House bought out the lease in 1836, Phillips's descendants received £170,468 in compensation.

In 1800, winter storms were at their worst and the two keepers were cut off for over four months. Relief ships approached the rock, in vain but at last one returned with the news that a man had been seen standing in the corner of the outer gallery with a distress flag. Every night the light shone, but when relief came at last the keeper was quite mad and his companion dead. The keeper, afraid to commit his dead friend to the sea in case he was accused of murdering him, had tied his body to the gallery railing. Henceforward three keepers were appointed to the rock lighthouse.

In 1801 Robert Stevenson found the lighthouse in a distressing state. The light was badly kept and the reflectors almost worn out so that rather than being the most important light in the local group the Smalls was the worst. On a second visit, in 1818, he found eighteen reflectors completely filling the small lantern room The lighthouse was damaged by storm in 1831, when the floor and two sides of the cabin were wrecked, leaving the keepers in the lantern room fearing for their lives.

In 1859, Trinity House proposed the building of a new lighthouse on the Smalls. Chief engineer Sir James Douglass designed a handsome tower of granite. The stones were prepared on shore, and the report of the royal commissioners stated:

> Each stone has a square hollow on each edge, and a square hole in the centre; when set in its place, a wedge of slate called 'a joggle' fits into the square opening formed by joining the two upper stones. The joint is placed exactly over the centre of the under stone, into which the joggle is wedged before the two upper stones are placed. The result is, that each set of three stones is fastened together by a fourth, which acts as a pin to keep the tiers from sliding on each other. The base of the building is solid. Two iron cranes slide up an iron pillar in the middle,

and are fixed by pins at the required position as the work advances. The two are used together, so as to obviate any inequality of strain.

The station is serviced by helicopter from Swansea.

Established 1778 (present tower 1861)
Height of light above MHW 126ft
Height of tower 141ft
Range 26 miles
W Gp Fl (15sec), 552,000cp
Optic 1st order catadioptric
Electricity, 240V 400W
    (mercury iodide burner)
Supertyfon fog horns (60sec) 2 blasts
No public access

SKOKHOLM

Walkers on the Pembrokeshire Coast Path in the region of St Ann's Head will see the lighthouse on Skokholm Island, a bird sanctuary about five miles offshore. The station was built to the design of

Skokholm: the compact, architecturally unusual light is situated on an island bird sanctuary

Sir Thomas Matthews and established during World War I.

Before construction could start a jetty had to be built; supplies were taken from the jetty to the site by a mile-long narrow gauge railway in trucks originally pulled by a donkey, then a pony. The animals learned to hide when their services were required on relief days, it is recorded. A tractor was subsequently used for haulage, when relief was by tender from Holyhead, but a helicopter is now used.

The keepers on Skokholm are rarely alone; scientists and students are frequent visitors to the bird sanctuary.

Established 1916
Height of light above MHW 177ft
Height of tower 58ft
Range 19.6 miles
R Fl (10sec), 100,000cp
Optic 4th order catadioptric
Electricity, 100V 1,000W
Supertyfon fog horns (15sec)
Open to public by appointment only

ST ANN'S HEAD

The approach to Milford Haven, one of Britain's finest natural deep-water harbours, is by the hazardous Crow Rock and the Toes off Linney Head. Merchants and shipowners have for centuries recognised the importance of Milford Haven and the harbour has grown increasingly busy; as early as the seventeenth century, Trinity House approved a coal-fired light on St Ann's Head to guide Milford-bound shipping. It was to be supported by voluntary dues, but the owners of the light exacted payments illegally and it was closed down. At the time, it was the only light on the west coast. No other was kindled for over forty years until Trinity House was granted a patent for a light on the same spot and, early in the eighteenth century, leased it to the owner of the land, Joseph Allen. He agreed to build and maintain two lighthouses, collecting dues at Milford Haven of one penny per ton cargo on British and twopence on foreign vessels.

Robert Stevenson visited the station in 1801 and described the

St Ann's Head: one of Britain's earliest west-coast stations

towers as leading lights. Also:

> The light is from Argand burners with parabolic silvered copper reflectors each twenty and a half inches in diameter. In the one lantern there are sixteen reflectors and in the other eleven, and though they are only about one hundred paces distant from each other there is a distinct keeper at each lantern, so that they are in the most complete state of cleanliness and good order.

The rear light was closed down in 1910 and is now a coastguard station, passed on the way to the present lighthouse which is reached from the village of Dale.

Established 1714 (present tower 1841)
Height of light above MHW 159ft
Height of tower 42ft
Range 18.9 miles
W R Fl (5sec), 333,000cp
Optic 1st order catadioptric
Electricity, 240V 3,000W
Tannoy fog horns (60sec) 2 blasts
Open to public

CALDY ISLAND

Caldy Island is familiar to Tenby holidaymakers, many of whom visit the monastery there. The island was given to the Benedictines by the abbey of Tiron, in France, in 1131 but they were expelled in 1536. Four centuries later, in 1906, an Anglican Benedictine brotherhood bought the island and built the monastery, selling it in the early 1920s to the present incumbents, the Order of Reformed Cistercians.

The lighthouse stands on the summit of Caldy; the designer was a Trinity House engineer and the total cost of the construction work was £3,380. Originally manned by keepers who lived on the station with their families, the light is now automatic.

> Established 1829
> Height of light above MHW 214ft
> Height of tower 52ft
> Range 21 miles
> W R Gp Fl (20sec), 10,000cp
> Optic 2nd order catadioptric
> Acetylene
> No public access

Caldy Island: the lighthouse is unmanned but Tenby's holidaymakers visit it by pleasure boat

MUMBLES

The lighthouse, on the outer of two islets at the western end of Swansea Bay, is a local light maintained by the British Transport Dock Board. Its principal function is to guide shipping safely into Swansea Bay past the Mumbles, a small group of rocks.

Swansea Town Council received permission to build a lighthouse and keepers' dwellings on Mumbles Head at the end of the eighteenth century, the lease to run for ninety-nine years at an annual rent of £5. A stone tower with two coal fires was built, one fire set several feet above the other, but it was not long before Argand lamps and reflectors were installed. At about the same time (1803) a small pierhead light was erected at Swansea.

Trinity House failed in a bid to buy up the remainder of the Mumbles lease and it was secured in 1835 by the Swansea harbour authorities who, for the fifty years they maintained the light, made only £6,000 profit.

Established 1794
Height of light above MHW 114ft
Height of tower 56ft
Range 19 miles
W Gp Fl (10sec)
Electricity
Diaphone fog signal (60sec) 3 blasts
No public access

NASH POINT

This lighthouse was built to mark sandbanks off the point following a public outcry after the wreck of the passenger steamer *Frolic* in 1830, with heavy loss of life. Two towers were built, set 330yd apart as leading lights to indicate a safe passage past the sandbanks; the low light was abandoned early this century. The high light was electrified in 1971.

Established 1832
Height of light above MHW 184ft
Height of tower 122ft
Range 19.5 miles

W R Fl (10sec), 146,000cp
Optic 1st order catadioptric
Electricity, 240V 1,500W
Fog sirens (45sec) 2 blasts
Open to public

FLATHOLM

The island of Flatholm lies centrally in the shipping lanes where the
Bristol Channel meets the Severn estuary. The Severn at this point
is a busy river, where ships to and from Cardiff, Newport, Bristol
and Gloucester pass frequently.

The Society of Merchant Venturers of Bristol discussed the establishment of a light in the seventeenth century but Trinity House was
not petitioned until 1733. The first petitioner, John Eldridge, was
rejected but William Crispe was successful some years later. A coal-
fired light was specified.

*Flatholm: this light serves the ports of the Severn Estuary; holidaymakers on
both sides of the water are familiar with Flatholm island's low profile*

Crispe and his partner Benjamin Lund built a strong tower and a fire was lit, but they were bankrupted by the expense and forced to sell their lease.

Complaints about the quality of the light were frequent, and a proposal was made in 1816 that gas jets forming the shape of an anchor should be tried. It was not adopted, and Trinity House agreed to rebuild and maintain the station for the remainder of the lease, raising the tower and fitting Argand burners and reflectors which came into operation here in 1820. Further improvements took place in 1825, 1867, 1923 and 1969 when the station was electrified.

A lighthouse and wreck can be seen on a memorial in Bristol Cathedral to George Robinson, 'drowned by the upsetting of a boat while crossing the channel from the island of Flatholm where he was superintending the improvement of the lighthouse under the direction of the Honourable Corporation of Trinity House'.

Established 1737 (present tower 1820)
Height of light above MHW 164ft
Height of tower 99ft
Range 19 miles
W R Gp Fl (10sec), 139,000cp
Optic 1st order catadioptric
Electricity, 240V 1,500W
Fog siren (30sec)
Open to public

EAST USK

With the rise in importance of Newport (Gwent), navigation lights became necessary at the mouth of the river Usk through which the port is approached. A lighthouse tower was built on the west bank in 1821, but was closed down about eighty years later when Trinity House commissioned a tower on the eastern side of the river entrance. This lighthouse is reached through the village of Nash and along the sea bank. The tower, within a walled compound, stands on six screw piles sunk 15½ft into the ground. The piles were encased in concrete between 1954 and 1961 when deposits of ash slurry from Uskmouth power station raised the ground level by thirteen feet.

Established 1893
Height of light above MHW 36ft
Height of tower 44ft
Range 15 miles (W), 11 miles (R and G)
W R G Gp Fl (10sec), 13,000cp
Optic 4th order dioptric
Electricity, 50V 250W
No public access (unwatched)

BLACKNORE POINT

Blacknore Point lighthouse was built by Trinity House to assist
shipping moving into and out of the docks at Avonmouth on the
river Severn north-west of Bristol; it is similar to East Usk in construction. To reach the lighthouse, it is necessary to travel from
Portishead to Nore Cottage on the Clevedon road, thence by private
road to Blacknore Farm and footpath to the tower.

There are no dwellings or outbuildings: the tower stands alone.

Established 1894
Height of light above MHW 36ft
Height of tower 36ft
Range 11.3 miles
W Gp Fl (10sec), 12,000cp (W),
  2,500cp (R and G)
Optic 4th order biform dioptric
Electricity, 230V 100W
No public access (unwatched)

BURNHAM-ON-SEA

A fisherman's wife of Burnham is reputed to be the originator of
the light there; she kept a candle in the window of her cottage as a
beacon for the local fleet and agreed to maintain it after her hus-
band's death by drowning. Later, the sexton of St Andrew's church
showed a light from the church tower in spite of the unchristian
disapproval of his bishop for the humane act.

By the early nineteenth century the port of Bridgwater was
flourishing and Trinity House granted a lease for a permanent light

to Rev David Davies, the curate. He prospered, not surprisingly because the dues were five shillings for British ships, ten shillings for foreign, and three shillings for coastal vessels. Trinity House paid £16,000 for the lease in 1829.

Burnham-on-Sea: the leading lights with their broad red stripes (front light disused)

A pair of leading lights was built three years later to guide shipping into the river Parrett, the approach to Bridgwater. The high light is still in use but the low light, which had deteriorated structurally, was closed in 1969 and replaced by a new light at Huntspill about two miles away.

Established 1832
Height of light above MHW 91ft
Height of tower 99ft
Range 17 miles
W Occ (7.5sec), 40,000cp
Optic 1st order catadioptric
Electricity, 100V 1,000W
No public access (unwatched)

LYNMOUTH FORELAND

There is a clifftop walk to the foreland along a path from the old inn near Countisbury. It is a long and impressive route along the headland and round the cliffs to the lighthouse, at times reaching 500ft and giving magnificent views. Grass gives way to a well-worn footpath along the very side of the cliff, and after about two miles the track starts descending to the lighthouse on the point, well below the crest of the headland. The walk is never really dangerous provided care is taken. There is a lighthouse service road from the A39 which makes for an easy but less spectacular visit.

Lynmouth Foreland: this unusual station is built on the side of a cliff about 200ft above the sea

The height of the station above the sea is an immediate explanation of the short tower, and its compactness is dictated by its situation.

Established 1900
Height of light above MHW 220ft
Height of tower 16ft
Range 21.4 miles
W Gp Fl (15sec), 168,000cp
Optic 1st order catadioptric
Electricity, 240V 400W
Electric fog horn (30sec) 3 blasts
Open to public

ILFRACOMBE

Many coastal churches and chapels maintained navigational lights, among them St Catherine's (Isle of Wight), Boston, and Blakeney and Winterton in Norfolk; a document of 1585 states that danger to shipping off the East Anglian coast might be reduced 'iffe a contynuall lighte were maynteyned uppon the steeple of Winterton'. The Bishop of Exeter granted an indulgence as early as 1522 for the

Ilfracombe: one of the few church towers still incorporating a lantern

maintenance of a light on the roof of a chapel overlooking Ilfracombe harbour, and priests kept the wood fire burning through the winter months; it shone like a 'twinkling star', according to a contemporary account.

Today, the chapel on Lantern Hill still shows a light from 1 September to 30 March (R F, range 6 miles) at a height of 127ft above the sea. Storm signals are hoisted on the tower when appropriate.

BULL POINT

Bull Point lighthouse forms a corner of a triangle of lights based on Lundy and Hartland Point. It is sited on a plateau open to the sea on three sides, and the visitor can look down on the station.

Cliff-face erosion is a problem in this area and evidence of landslips is to be seen. In 1972 part of the plateau collapsed into the sea, irreparably damaging the fog signal house and endangering the tower to such an extent that it had to be abandoned. Trinity House erected a temporary tower to hold the apparatus from the old tower. A new station is scheduled for 1976, and the old buildings will be demolished.

Bull Point: coastal erosion made the station dangerous and Trinity House was obliged to use a temporary structure after the collapse of the fog signal house

161

Established 1879 (new station 1976)
Height of light above MHW 154ft
Height of tower 55ft
Range 18.6 miles
W Gp Fl (10sec), 800,000cp
Optic small 3rd order catadioptric
Electricity, 100V, 1,500W
Diaphone fog horns (60sec)
No public access

LUNDY

Lundy Island lies in the Bristol Channel about twelve miles off the coast of north Devon. It is a rugged place, surrounded by rocks and difficult to approach without local knowledge. The island has about twenty miles of coastline, much of it potentially dangerous, and Trinity House recognised this in 1819 when they proposed and later built a lighthouse on Chapel Hill. Two lights were shown, the upper a quick-flashing white light, an optical innovation at that

Lundy South: this station, and its Lundy North companion, are serviced from Swansea by helicopter

Lundy North

time which did not achieve complete success. The Lundy optic
revolved so quickly that no appreciable periods of darkness were
noticeable between the flashes; in any case, from a distance of
five miles the upper and lower lights appeared to merge into one.

This misleading characteristic led to a tragedy when *La Jeune
Emma,* en route to Cherbourg, mistook the Lundy light for the
fixed light at Ushant and went aground on the rocks.

The lighthouse was abandoned in 1897 and two new towers
built, one on the northern and the other on the southern extremity
of the island. Both are fully manned but the northern station holds
electronic equipment which can be controlled from the other
lighthouse. A Swansea-based helicopter services the Lundy estab-
lishments. Visitors may sail from Ilfracombe and there are
seasonal boat trips from several Bristol Channel resorts. Landing
is not always possible, but there are usually good views to be had
of Lundy South.

Lundy	Established c1820 (present tower 1897)
North	Height of light above MHW 165ft
	Height of tower 56ft
	Range 24 miles
	W Gp Fl (20sec), 860,000cp
	Optic 4th order PRB 20 sealed beam unit
	Electricity, 50V 250W
	Tannoy fog horns (30sec) Mo(N)
	Open to public
Lundy	Established c1820 (present tower 1897)
South	Height of light above MHW 175ft
	Height of tower 52ft
	Range 19.4 miles
	W Fl (5sec), 576,000cp
	Optic 4th order catadioptric
	Electricity, 100V 1,000W
	Supertyfon fog horns (25sec)
	Open to public

HARTLAND POINT

The scenery of this part of north-west Devon is dramatic, with high, sheer cliffs and far-reaching views.

The lighthouse, built by Trinity House on a large rock at the tip of the point, was threatened by the undermining action of the sea to such an extent that rock had to be broken from the cliff head behind the lighthouse to fall on the beach and form a barrier against the waves. Tons of boulders fell but were washed away, although they had the desired effect of slowing undercliff erosion, and the procedure had to be repeated at intervals of a year to a year and a half. Eventually it became necessary to construct a permanent barrier, and a sea wall 130ft long and 19ft high was built in 1925.

Hartland Point belongs to the National Trust and a car park is provided at the start of the cliff walk to the lighthouse, which is revealed suddenly as the walker approaches.

Established 1874
Height of light above MHW 120ft

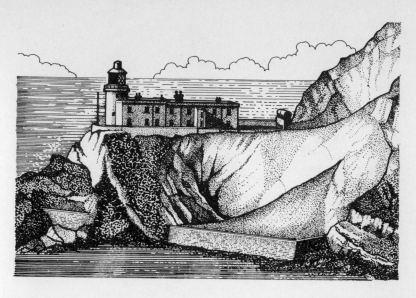

Hartland Point: the spectacular cliff setting in National Trust land attracts visitors to the station

Height of tower 59ft
Range 17 miles
W Gp Fl (15sec), 1,250,000cp
Optic 3rd order biform catadioptric
Electricity, 100V 3,500W
Diaphone fog signals (75secs) 3 blasts
Open to public

TREVOSE HEAD

A lighthouse on the head was proposed first in 1809 and sub-sequently in 1813 and 1832, but none was built until a further fifteen years had passed, which is surprising in view of the fact that the only other lights at that time in the busy Bristol Channel were Lundy and Longships. Even more surprising is the decision to dispense with a fog signal in an area which is prone to fog.

The old optic was replaced during modernisation in 1882, and the light source in 1922, when the newly developed Hood vaporised oil burner with an autoform mantle was installed (an autoform mantle

Trevose Head: the enormous fog signal (left), now replaced, was in use for many years

assumes a spherical shape). This burner was still in use when electrification trials took place in 1973.

Lord Rayleigh, scientific adviser to Trinity House 1896-1919, successfully developed a gigantic fog signal which was used in experiments at Trevose Head. It was shaped like an enormous trumpet, 36ft long and rectangular in section, and emitted a wide horizontal spread of powerful sound.

Established 1847
Height of light above MHW 204ft
Height of tower 87ft
Range 25 miles
R Fl (5sec), 198,000cp
Optic 1st order catadioptric
Electricity, 240V 1,000W
Supertyfon fog horns (30sec) 2 blasts
Open to public

GODREVY ISLAND

Holidaymakers at St Ives and Penzance used to take part in a traditional Whit Monday steamer excursion to Godrevy lighthouse, and their modern counterparts will be familiar with the view of the island across St Ives Bay.

Godrevy lighthouse was built following the outcry upon the loss in 1854 of the passenger steamer *Nile* with all aboard. The ship ploughed into the Stones, an unlit reef stretching into St Ives Bay, and the tragedy stimulated action which culminated five years later in the construction of the new seamark.

Godrevy Island: traditional Whit Monday excursions were made by visitors from Penzance and St Ives to this island light

The white octagonal tower is of rubble stone bedded in mortar, and is situated with its dwelling on a large rock. Alterations in 1939 involved the installation of a new optic and light source and the full automation of the station, after which the keepers were withdrawn.

A wind generator, tested at Dungeness, has been installed, making Godrevy unique among British lights.

Established 1859
Height of light above MHW 120ft
Height of tower 86ft
Range 17 miles
W R Fl (10sec), 27,000cp
Optic 2nd order catadioptric
Wind Generator 32V 250W
No public access (unwatched)

PENDEEN

The coast from Gurnard's Head to Cape Cornwall is rugged, with rocks extending out to sea, and the Pendeen light was built to guide shipping past the Wra Stones off the head.

The beacon was established here in the sixteenth century, tended by a hermit, and the antiquary John Leland (1506?-52) observed here a 'chapel of St Nicholas and a pharos for a light for ships sailing by night in these quarters'. St Nicholas was a favourite saint of seafarers, and many coastal churches and chapels are dedicated to him. The beacon disappeared at the Dissolution of the Monasteries

Pendeen: a beautiful situation on Cornwall's western peninsula

(1536-40) and Leland's is the only record of the early light.

The present lighthouse, established at the turn of the century and built to the design of Sir Thomas Matthews, a Cornishman, is reached from St Just; there is parking space on the headland. The tower, built of rubble stone rendered with cement mortar, and white-painted, commands a situation which is one of the most picturesque in England and Wales.

Established 1900
Height of light above MHW 195ft
Height of tower 56ft
Range 20.4 miles
W Gp Fl (15sec), 2,000,000cp
Optic 1st order dioptric
Electricity, 100V 3,500W
Fog siren (20sec)
Open to public

Lighthouses Open to the Public

These lighthouses are open to the public free of charge from 1pm until one hour before sunset every day except Sunday or during fog, without prior permission from Trinity House. Work may be in progress at any time and visits are subject to the convenience of the service; parties should check with the principal keeper in order to avoid disappointment. No risk, responsibility or expense is accepted by Trinity House in connection with a visit.

Alderney	Principal Keeper, Alderney Lighthouse, Alderney, Channel Islands	Alderney 08 2522
Anvil Point	Principal Keeper, Anvil Point Lighthouse, Swanage, Dorset	Swanage 2146
Bardsey Island	Principal Keeper, Bardsey Lighthouse, c/o Aberdaron Post Office, Pwllheli, Gwynedd	
Cromer	Principal Keeper, Cromer Lighthouse, Cromer, Norfolk	Cromer 2123
Calf of Man	*see* Isle of Man	
Douglas Head	*see* Isle of Man	
Dungeness (base only)	Principal Keeper, Dungeness Lighthouse, Romney Marsh, Lydd, Kent	Lydd 20236 and 20262

Flamborough	Principal Keeper, Flamborough Lighthouse, near Bridlington, North Humberside	Flamborough 345
Flatholm	Principal Keeper Flatholm Lighthouse, c/o The Superintendent, Trinity House Depot, Swansea	via Barry 2925 Coastguard - OGG 62 2925
Great Ormes Head	Principal Keeper, Great Ormes Head Lighthouse, Llandudno, Gwynedd	Llandudno 76819
Hartland Point	Principal Keeper, Hartland Point Lighthouse, Bideford, North Devon	Hartland 328
Isle of Man (all stations)	Principal Keeper, Isle of Man Lighthouse,	
Langness	*see* Isle of Man	
Lizard	Principal Keeper, Lizard Lighthouse, The Lizard, Helston, Cornwall	Lizard 231
Lowestoft	Principal Keeper, Lowestoft Lighthouse, Lowestoft, Suffolk	Lowestoft 3034
Lundy North	Lundy Island, c/o GPO, Bideford, North Devon (summertime only)	Mumbles Coastguard - Swansea 66534
Lundy South	c/o The Superintendent Trinity House Depot, Swansea	Swansea 66534 (phone link between lighthouses)

Lynmouth Foreland	Principal Keeper, Lynmouth Foreland Lighthouse, Lynton, North Devon	Brendon 226
Manghold Head	*see* Isle of Man	
Nash Point	Principal Keeper, Nash Point Lighthouse, Llantwit Major, South Glamorgan	Llantwit Major 3471
North Foreland	Principal Keeper, North Foreland Lighthouse, near Broadstairs, Kent	Thanet 61869
Pendeen	Principal Keeper, Pendeen Lighthouse, Pendeen, Cornwall	St Just 418
Penlee Point Fog Signal	Principal Keeper, Fog Station, Penlee, Plymouth PL10 1LW	Millbrook 460
Point of Ayre	*see* Isle of Man	
Point Lynas	Principal Keeper, Point Lynas Lighthouse, Amlwch, Gwynedd	Amlwch 333
Portland Bill	Principal Keeper, Portland Bill Lighthouse, Easton, Portland, Dorset	Portland 020495
Sark	Principal Keeper, Sark Lighthouse, Sark, Channel Islands	Sark 21
Skerries	Principal Keeper, Skerries Lighthouse, c/o The Superintendent, Trinity House Depot, Holyhead, Gwynedd	Holyhead 2329 and 2320

172

Skokholm Island	Principal Keeper, Skokholm Island Lighthouse, c/o The Superintendent, Trinity House Depot, Holyhead, Gwynedd	
Souter Point	Principal Keeper, Souter Point Lighthouse, Whitburn Collieries, Sunderland, Tyne and Wear	Whitburn 3161
South Stack	Principal Keeper, South Stack Lighthouse, c/o The Superintendent, Trinity House Depot, Holyhead, Gwynedd	Holyhead 2042
Start Point	Principal Keeper, Start Point Lighthouse, Hallsands, near Kingsbridge, North Devon	Torcross 225
St Ann's Head	Principal Keeper, St Ann's Head Lighthouse, Dale, Haverfordwest, Dyfed	Dale 314
St Anthony	Principal Keeper, St Anthony Lighthouse, Portscatho, Cornwall	Portscatho 213
St Bees	Principal Keeper, St Bees Lighthouse, Sandwich, Whitehaven, Cumberland	Whitehaven 2635
St Catherine's	Principal Keeper, St Catherine's Lighthouse, Niton, Undercliffe, Ventnor, Isle of Wight	Niton 284

St Mary's Island	Principal Keeper, St Mary's Island Lighthouse, Whitley Bay, Tyne and Wear	Whitley Bay 25077
Strumble Head	Principal Keeper, Strumble Head Lighthouse, Goodwick, Pembrokeshire, Dyfed	St Nicholas 258
Trevose	Principal Keeper, Trevose Lighthouse, St Merryn, near Padstow, Cornwall	St Merryn 494
Whitby	Principal Keeper, Whitby Lighthouse, Whitby, North Yorkshire	Whitby 2296
Withernsea	Principal Keeper, Withernsea Lighthouse, Withernsea HU19 2DY, North Humberside	Withernsea 2243

Bibliography

Adams, W.H.D. *The Story of Our Lighthouses and Lightships* (Nelson, 1891)

Admiralty List of Lights, Vol A (Hydrographers of the Navy) regular updated editions

Armstrong, W. *White for Danger* (Elek, 1963)

Blake, G. *Clyde Lighthouses* (Jackson Son & Co, Glasgow, 1956)

Bowen, J.P. *British Lighthouses* (Longmans Green, 1947)

Chadwick, L. *Lighthouses and Lightships* (Dobson, 1971)

Cobb, J.F. *Watchers of the Longships* (Wells Gardener Darton 1952)

Encyclopaedia Britannica (various editions)

Goldsmith, G. C. *Looming Lights, The Goodwin Sands* (Constable, 1947 and 1953)

Majdalany, F. *The Red Rocks of Eddystone* (Longmans, 1962)

Phillips, G. W. *Lighthouses and Lightship* (Rolls House Publishing Co, 1949)

Stevenson, D. A. *English Lighthouse Tours 1801-1813-1818* Nelson, 1946); *The World's Lighthouses Before 1820* (OUP, 1959)

Talbot, E. A. *Lighthouses and Lightships* (Heinemann, 1913)

Wryde, S. *The Lighthouses of Great Britain* (Ernest Benn, 1913)

REPORTS, ETC

Smeaton, J. *Eddystone Lighthouse* (1791)

Stevenson, A. *Skerryvore Lighthouse, with Notes on Lighthouse Illumination* (1848)

Stevenson, D. *Lighthouses* (1864)

Stevenson, R. *Bell Rock Lighthouse* (1824)

Stevenson, T. *Lighthouse Construction and Illumination* (1881)

Acknowledgements

The author would like to express thanks to the following:
Mr Hugh Collinson for information; the Corporation of Trinity
House for help, information and checking the text; Mr Albert
Hopkins who cycled the coast of the Isle of Man to obtain photo-
graphs; the Humber Conservancy Board; Dr Gordon Jackson (the
author's brother) for editorial assistance; Stuart McLain who visited
St Mary's Island on the author's behalf; the Northern Lighthouse
Board for information on the Manx lighthouses; the Port of Sunder-
land Authority; the Royal Air Force, Valley; and the many keepers
who provided first-hand information.